MW01688158

Bedside Matters

BEDSIDE MATTERS

Thanks for listening

DOMINICK ACQUARO, M.D.

Venados Publishing

Published by Venados Publishing
2510 East Dupont Road, Suite 238, Fort Wayne, Indiana 46825

Printed in the United States of America
ISBN (paperback) 0-9669442-0-8

Cover design by MMG Graphics
Editorial and production services by Griffith Publishing

Dedication

This book was a project that helped me heal and taught me how to understand and appreciate gain through loss. I've gained from those that I dedicate this book to. I've gained from a very special wife who excites me when I'm in her presence and when I think about her, just as much as she did on the day we first met. I've gained and continue to gain from my children, in order of their birth, Andrea, Amanda, Gabrielle and Dominick. I've gained from my parents and I thank them for being cool enough to keep the family together, by raising their kids as a team. I especially thank my mother for reading to me and showing me the value of reading. I can't remember a time when she wasn't reading. They are all greatly appreciated. And lastly, I've gained a volume from my patients and I thank them for allowing me the honor to serve them and to care for them. I dedicate this book with hopes that it will be accepted from my heart, to those who choose to read it.

Table of Contents

Dedication..v
Preface viii
Acknowledgments..xi
Did I Say Good-bye?....................................xii
Charlie Died Today 1
Don't Take Anything for Granted.................3
Mrs. W 5
I Have to Know 9
I Ain't Got No Education 13
SOS 19
I Hide My Hands...23
Wolves in Sheep's Clothing........................27
There is Quality in Dying 30
Norma 33
The Nature of Things 36
Gangrene Leg...39
Could You Imagine?....................................43
Wealth 47
Annie..51
Disability..54
Why Did I Ever Get Old? 57
Sara 61
My Task..67
Leon 73
Helga..81

I'm Really Sick 83
Gimmicks 87
I Just Had To Do It 93
It's My Turn 97
My Wild Irish Rose 101
Miss Rowdy's the Nurse For Me 103
The Ninety-Year-Old Sisters Who
Watched TV and Never Talked 107
Burn Patients Want to Survive 109
That's Easy For You to Say 113
What You See is What You Get 115
Do You Not Realize? 117
Staying on Time 121
No, I'm Not Really Scared 123
Hold On 127
First Day Back 131
You Must Have Been. 135
The Week I Was Ready to Quit 137
Please, Let the Doctor Diagnose 139
They Can't All Love You 141
It Just Seems Like Yesterday 145
I Have Enough to Eat 147
Sharing Our Gifts 148
The Downs Syndrome Child 153
The Last to Know 157
Where Did All the Used Station
Wagons Go? 161
Keith 165
Bob 169
I Didn't Realize 173

Preface

I cringe when I hear about anyone who takes innocence from a child. When people hear stories about bad things happening, it's a struggle for them not to believe that everyone is bad. It hurts me when I see a doctor take dignity from a patient.

Are all people bad? Is the entire world bad? Is bad good? Is one person bad but someone else is good? Why on earth would someone take innocence away from another? Where has America gone? To the dogs? When people have bad experiences, they usually can't wait to tell a ton of people, yet when something good happens, only a few people hear about it.

How often do we hear about a good marriage where a family man hurries home to care for his family, doing all of the right things for them? We don't. But, we often hear stories about the dirty, lowdown scoundrels who leave their families high and dry. Which stories would we rather hear? Probably the bad ones. In our society today we prefer hearing the bad news over the good news. Sadly, stories about bad individuals inundate our homes every night on the evening news while stories about people who do good things only get seasonal credit.

Occasionally, we will hear about a deserving hero on the news, but, more often than not, the stories we hear are about someone who has crossed the line. When a professional crosses the line, all the others in the same profession feels like they need to prove that they are not bad.

I saw a priest on the news one evening saying, "I cannot hold a child and share love, because I fear it will be taken the wrong way." When a millionaire crosses the line, the tone is set for many people to destroy him or her, because it is time for the have-nots to have their turn. Who sets the tone and why would anyone set the tone in such a fashion? Who gains from any of this?

When a doctor does something wrong, it tends to make all doctors feel that they've been labeled bad. When a star athlete takes drugs, people will most assuredly believe that all athletes are doing the same thing. Who sets the stage for the battle between all of us? Who gains from bad stories? No one. Each of us loses something.

This book contains experiences I have had in the medical profession, because that is my profession. I've seen losses on both sides. I've seen patients lose confidence in competent physicians, and I've seen physicians lose confidence in patients, which sometimes makes it a struggle to keep going. It shouldn't be this way, but it is, although, of course, there are exceptions to everything.

Over a short period of time in my medical practice I have come up with stories that probably wouldn't make the evening news. Some of them would not even make it past my computer screen. The stories in this book reflect the way I feel and, I believe, how other physicians feel. I hurt when my patients hurt, and I care for the patients that have come my way. I feel fortunate that they have chosen me to care for them. These stories were written from my heart. The people I write about have touched me forever, and hence have allowed me to grow.

Acknowledgements

When I was attending college I wrote a term paper, placed as many commas as I could possibly get into each page—and received a poor mark for my efforts. I was told by my professor that I had good things to say, but somehow I had let little things take away the good things. This entire project was heading to the waste management deposit until one day, right under my nose, I had the answer and it was from a patient. Carol Burris had the incredible talent I needed to save this project and she came to my rescue. She herself is a talented published author who encouraged me to proceed on with my goal, and through her editing and removal of commas, she gave me a chance to present this book, with the anticipation of not receiving a poor mark.

Did I Say Good-bye?

Get up early.
Read your books and journals.
If you're tired, you can watch the news.
You know the news is always on.
Does it really matter what time of day?
Damn, it's late!
Gotta do my walking.
The tape's on and I'm learning as I
walk.
Eat breakfast.
It's good to eat breakfast.
Kiss my wife.
Kiss my kids.
Say good-bye.
What if I never said good-bye?
Would something bad happen, if I never
said good-bye?
Work, work, work.
Drive, drive, slow down, wonder, look,
don't see.
Pick another route, something
happened.
I pray my family is safe.
Thank God.
Repeat the above.
Get to work on a different day.
Oh, my God!

When I began my medical practice I had a computer program that gave each of my patients a number. This made it easy for the office staff and myself to identify them, and that helped me in more ways than

I could have even imagined. I was happy to finally be a practicing physician, in my own office.

I started seeing patients before I had even finished unpacking, so my office was a mess. There were boxes stacked in every corner and clutter everywhere. When my patient entered my office, he looked pretty spiffy. He was wearing a bow tie and was acting like he owned the place. I was comfortable with this, because the gentleman had a kindness about him that exuded through what could have easily been misconstrued as arrogance. Hell, he wasn't even Italian. He chatted with me for a while and informed me that I was going to be his doctor, because his wife was already my patient. Suddenly I recalled who my number one patient had been—his wife. I began with my usual physical checkup procedure, which included having him strip down to his shorts.

Through the years I have taken care of this very nice man and his wife and I grew to like for the two of them very much. They had traveled the globe and told me interesting stories I probably would have never heard, if not for their extensive travels. The wife was sicker than the husband, and they rarely came to my office without the other.

Every now and then, the nice gentleman would remind me that he was my number two patient and we had a lot of fun with that remark. As the years rolled on, when it seemed appropriate, I would make a house call, so I could be sure that the fine lady was being properly cared for medically. The woman would always ask me intelligent medical questions and twenty percent of the time, she did what I advised her to do.

Every day before I left home for my day's work, I would go through my morning ritual, as my poem says. It's my disposition to worry too much that something bad might happy to my family, because I'm overly protective of them. One particular day when I was heading home from work on my usual I-69 Route, I ran into a traffic jam because there had been an accident. I prayed that my family was OK. When I finally did arrive home, rather late, I was happy and thankful that my wife and kids were all intact, safe and well, just as I had left them. The next morning when I walked into my office, I was presented with the bad news that my number two's number one had perished in the accident that had caused the traffic jam the evening before. The woman was a wonderful person and a cherished patient of mine.

I immediately called her daughter to tell her how sorry I was and I told her to give the family my best. I will truly miss my number two's number one, because they had both managed to melt a place in my heart that will always be remembered. God bless both of their souls.

Charlie Died Today

He was the neighbor next door that I never
had.
One I never had but would have liked to have.
I would have liked that very much.
Charlie is such an easy name.
He was a good guy, but he was never my
neighbor.
I really liked Charlie.
Everyone liked Charlie because he did what he
set out to do.
I pulled one way, he pulled another.
Why do they shoot horses, anyway?

Charlie died today. He was such a neat patient. I loved Charlie. I loved taking care of Charlie. I never wanted him to die. Charlie came to me a few years ago with Parkinson's disease and he hated the fact that he was not in control of his body. Even though he was filled with disgust because he could not make his body go in the direction in which he pointed it, he was still able to make everyone laugh. He was simply Charlie. What a great name.

We had some very nice office visits and on the days when he felt good he would announce to everyone, "Charlie's here!" Those were the days when he would walk into the office acting like he was fully in charge.

Charlie became very ill, and I had to admit him into the hospital. I did everything medically possible to hold on to Charlie. Hell, I didn't want to lose him. He was a nice man and taught me a lot. Only this time he was taking from me. I didn't have to look very hard at him to realize that Charlie had given up.

I'm sad for me that Charlie died today.

I just now got back from the hospital where I spent some very nice moments with Charlie's wife and their daughters he left behind. They told me some stories that made me wish I had known Charlie forever. He was such a good man. I loved Charlie and will miss him terribly, but I'm happy for Charlie that he doesn't have to suffer anymore.

Don't Take Anything for Granted

I learned a lesson a long time ago that the saying, "Actions speak louder than words," just ain't necessarily so.

While I was working in the burn center of a hospital, I learned that the patients there are as frightened as anyone could ever imagine. Before burn patients enter a hospital, they most likely have been doing great, physically. Then suddenly they are facing a potentially life-threatening condition, and this causes them much stress.

Added to that is the stress of seeing all the activity among the staff caring for them as they hurry and scurry about, talking in codes, almost forgetting that their patients are even there.

One of my burn patients was an elderly lady who was very frightened. I put my hand on her shoulder and said to her, "We are doing everything we possibly can to help you."

She was sobbing and for the life of me, I could not figure out how something so horrible could have happened to her. Her eyes looked directly into mine, which made me feel very uncomfortable. I wanted to ease her mind and once again, I reminded her of my intentions, and said, "Ma'am, I'm going to take good care of you here." Within seconds, her face radiated with relief and she couldn't stop thanking me for telling her that I would take care of her.

Doctors are trained to take care of their patients, but they are not trained to tell the patients that they will. I do not tell all of my patients the same thing, but since that time I have tried to tell them in one way or another that I will take care of them. I try to set my patients at ease as much as possible. That elderly woman taught me how to be a better caregiver, and I am grateful for the lesson I learned.

Mrs. W

I'm not paying my bill.
You don't have to.
Well, I'm not, so don't even think about
sending me a bill. You know why?
Yeah, I know why.
Why?
Cause you're not paying you're bill.
You're darn right I'm not paying. Hell, I'm
almost ninety. How do you expect me to
pay for you coming here to see me?
Obviously, I don't.
You can fire me as your patient, if you want.
Mrs. W, I'm not going to fire you and I'm not
going to send you a bill, OK?
OK. Did you know that I can play the
harmonica?
No ma'am, I didn't.
Well, I can.
Hey, you're good like that.
Now don't send me no bill. I'll come back and
bust you across the head. You hear me?
I hear you. Now get out of my office before I
pluck those gold teeth from your old, worn-
out head.
Now we understand each other. I like that.
Come see me in two months and we'll recheck
your medicine.

Dominick Acquaro, M.D.

Mrs. W showed up on the doorsteps at the entrance of my office in mild heart failure, not believing in doctors or the system. Well, that was OK. After taking medication for her condition, she soon was doing better.

We hit it off very well, right from the beginning. I was her lily white doctor. On our first meeting she said, "You know, I ain't never trusted a white man. No siree, and I ain't gonna start now."

After that statement, I knew I had my hands full, but I'm always up to a challenge. Every time Mrs. W comes in for an office visit, we begin our session cussing at each other, and then we get down to business. Mrs. W loves to cuss, and being an ex-sailor, I don't mind. I guess that's why we get along so well together.

One day when I was getting ready to finish an office visit, Mrs. W pulled the bills she had received from our office out of her purse and said, "I'm not going to pay these. Whatever the insurance pays is all you're ever gonna get, because I can't pay and I won't pay these bills."

I went out of the office to get Pat, who is the person in charge of the billing, and I brought her into the room. Mrs. W said, "you can bring in the U.S. Army, but I'm still not going to pay you."

I explained to Pat that we needed to take Mrs. W off of our billing records, and Mrs. W thanked me in her own way, by saying, "you sho'nuff betta, 'cause I ain't gonna pay you!"

I said, "You're welcome."

Every now and then Mrs. W brings me the best sweet potato pie you can ever imagine sinking your teeth into, so I figure that she's a little ahead on her payments with that.

Mrs. W came to me as a patient a few years ago, and I continue to take care of her. I saw her in November and she told me that her harmonica had broken, so I told her I would get her a new one for Christmas.

She could really play the harmonica. The first time I heard her she played "Amazing Grace" in our reception room in a way that would tear your heart right out of your chest. I bought Mrs. W a gold harmonica, the One Hundredth Anniversary Special Edition. I had been listening to her lungs and adjusting her treatment over the past few years, and she had been holding her own.

When I went to her house to give her the harmonica, she was as happy as a pig in sh--, but, when I heard her play, she wasn't the same harmonica player who had played in my reception room a few years before. Her heart had gotten worse. Enough to tell me that she was really struggling to get her songs out clearly.

I cut my visit short so that neither one of us would be forced to acknowledge that she didn't have the breath she needed to blow the harmonica. I gave her a big bear hug and wished her a great holiday and returned to my office. As soon as I got back, I reviewed her chart and read the cardiologist's notes that revealed her worsening condition.

Before then I had been preoccupied with thoughts of giving Mrs. W a new harmonica, which I didn't think she could afford. Hell. Maybe she could have; I hadn't even taken into account her heart setback. All I had been remembering was the great job she did playing "Amazing Grace" on the harmonica.

Mrs. W came into my office about a month later with two sweet potato pies. Neither of us mentioned anything about my visit to her home. I thanked her for the pies, gave her a big hug and told her to get out of my office before I called Security.

I heard her mumbling, underneath her breath, as she was leaving the office, “I’ll kick their a--if they think they can handle Mrs. W.”

I Have To Know

Well, I don't know about you.
What?
You know.
No, I don't.
Yeah, you're just sounding dumb, but I don't know.
I'll bet you do.
Maybe I do.
You do.
Would you be here if you thought I was dumb?
I got no choice much.
Sure you do.
Not much.
Sure you do.

A doctor-patient relationship is built on trust. Sometimes it happens on the very first visit, but there are those times when I never feel quite comfortable. I'm not a salesman, so I'm terrible at remembering names, but my patients never seem to mind. It's not as difficult when they come to my office, but when I'm out in public and I happen to see one of my patients, my mind draws a complete blank. I make sure that I chat with them for a while and let them know I appreciate their confidence in me as their physician.

When my patients come to me on their regular visits they question me indirectly through the stories they tell. Their questions are real, and they are always looking for a response, even though their questions may cover some tricky issues.

One day a lady came into my office and began telling me a story about an experience she had when she was a little girl. I had been doctoring her for a number of years and when she began telling me her story, I thought it was coming from out of nowhere. I had trouble trying to figure out what it was all about.

She told me that when she was a little girl she had done some chores for an uncle of hers and received a few coins from him. She grew up in poverty and knew nothing else, so those coins meant everything to her, even though they were burning a hole in her pocket. There was power in those coins for the short time she planned to keep them. She dreamed about how she was going to march into the Five-and-Dime dressed up in her best and spend those coins on whatever she pleased.

Her money was jingling in her pocket and pride filled the air as she bounced down the sidewalk, heading for the store. Nobody was going to stop that kid. Her stride quickened as she neared the dime store.

She started to lose her confidence, but that didn't stop her; she kept going. Her money gave her the power she needed to walk into the store and purchase what she wanted, knowing that soon she would be on her way back home whistling, "Sha boom, sha bang!"

Slowly and cautiously, she opened the door. It took all of the nerve she had, but she did it. She told me that everyone was staring at her and not in a cute way, either. They looked at her as if a Martian had entered the store.

Losing momentum, she quickly turned around and when she looked up, she saw the owner of the store looking directly at her with a frown on his face.

She said, "It's OK. I've got money." She went over to the candy case and picked out what she wanted and then went over to the counter to pay for it. She placed her cravings on the counter and as she looked around the store she saw a lot of people standing around as if they didn't have anything to do but to stare at a little girl buying candy.

Suddenly, she looked back at the cashier and felt like a hammer had come down on her, hard enough to break her apart. It ripped through her flesh as it made its way to the center of her soul. It tore and ripped inside of her with a mission and a passion of burning hell.

All of this clearly communicated the message to her, "We don't serve your kind around here. Now just run on."

She kept hearing the words, "Just run on," in her head.

She left the store, still clutching her money, and placed it in her pocket. She was hurting. She was ashamed for something that wasn't even her fault. She wondered if she should feel hate for her parents who had brought her into such a cruel world. She thought that the money in her pocket would have power, enough power to erase the color of her skin.

As I listened to my patient's sad story, I could see that she was an adult looking back, and I felt sympathy for an innocent child. She had gotten past most of the hurt, but not all of it, I knew, because if she had, what would have been her reason for telling me her story?

After all this time, I believe that she told me that story because she wanted to know if I was racially prejudiced. She wanted to put me through the test to see if I would accept her as my patient. She wanted to make very sure that I wanted to be her physician. There was no dancing through the hoops, or messin' round. She wanted to know the truth.

While she was telling me her story, she was getting her answer and was comforted. I continue to take care of the nice lady and relish the comfort I feel when she enters my office at each visit. I pride myself with this lady, because I can offer her a comfort zone.

On a few occasions I have felt that a good trusting relationship has been instantly formed, but on other occasions I do not feel as if I am in my comfort zone. It's always good to reach the comfort zone whereby I can have a doctor-patient relationship built on trust.

The story I've just told happens to be about the color of skin. It doesn't matter what color because there are so many. There are always people who need acceptance—the people we call foreigners and other labels. We need to lay down those hate issues or we the people are not really for the people. We can fly the flag all day, but if we go into our homes at night and teach our children to hate, shame on us. Don't just sing, "God Bless America." Do it!

I Ain't Got No Education

How long ya' been here?
Since '67.
What brought ya' here?
Didn't have no job, gotta work, ya' know?
I know.
Don't this cold weather get to ya' sometimes?
Sometimes.
Well, don't ya' miss the South, all nice and
  warm down there?
I do miss it, but ya' can't get no job if ya'
  ain't got no education.

I really enjoy being in the profession I have chosen. My patients touch me in many different ways. Many times I come out of the room after a visit and laugh about something we've made light of. The majority of my patients know that they can open up with me and do not feel in any way inhibited.

A few of the older patients take a while to realize that it's OK to be on a first name basis with me, but some of them do feel uncomfortable with that. The point I'm trying to make is that I'm OK with whatever they are OK with. My practice is so rewarding and enjoyable that I would take care of these nice people even if I didn't get paid for the privilege.

A few days ago one of my patients came to see me for a follow-up visit. He is a nice man but missing it somewhat when it comes to good grammar. (That don't bother me none, 'cause I feel that everyone can teach somebody something, and I've never known a diploma in hand to be a prerequisite for teaching.) I have been taking care of this man almost as long as I've been in practice. We chatted as usual, and I did my job as his physician and then told him I would again follow up on his condition in a few months.

While he was in my office he told me a story about how he had grown up in the South and had not gotten the full benefit of an education, for whatever reason.

I've heard some pretty good jokes, but I can almost never remember them well enough to tell them to someone else. But whenever anyone tells me a story that touches my heartstrings, it sticks to me like glue, and I can remember it forever.

Poverty is a bad thing, for whatever reason, but it never tears your heart out until you hear a story about children being involved.

When this patient was growing up, his mother told him that Santa Claus could come to see him only if there was snow on the ground because the reindeer could not land on anything but snow.

Now in his mid-fifties, he told me that he now understands about being poor and all the "why nots" in his life. There I was, looking at a mid-fifties man telling me his story with a face of a five-year-old pressing against a window pane, wondering if he could ever pray hard enough to make it snow, at least one year. I felt so bad for this child inside the body of a man that I didn't know what to do. I was overcome with sadness. My heart screamed silently. I felt helpless. How could I make up for the things that had been lost in a child?

Poverty is a bad thing, and the way a lot of us keep from feeling saddened by it is by blaming the victims. Somebody got pregnant, somebody dropped out of school, somebody did this, somebody did that. That gets us off the hook.

All I saw standing in my office that day was this child telling me his story from deep down inside the soul of a mid-fifties man. A child that no one would ever have another chance to touch, or help, to make things better.

No more comforting now. The hurting mid-fifties man was left to stand on his own. It was his job, and his job alone, to carry this child within himself, and his job alone, to find his comfort. I was deeply touched by this man's story and when I arrived home from my day's work, I shared it with my wife and she felt as saddened as I did.

My wife grew up in Mexico as a child of "haves" versus "have nots." Every year at Christmas her parents taught their children that it was the right thing to give gifts to the poor. The only problem was that they never saw the people who received the gifts. That kind of giving loses the personal touch.

She worked for a company in Chicago while I was in my residency and met a woman who has since become a dear and loving friend to our family. This woman is also from a small town in Mexico and was unfortunately one of the "have nots."

My wife had an easy time with the process of befriending her. My wife is a very dear and special caring person. I say that not because she dresses in leather, snapping a whip behind me, but because it is the truth.

She and her friend have shared many stories about Mexico since their meeting, and because of their common interest they have developed a neat friendship, which continues to grow.

My wife recalled a story a friend had told her up about how she grew up in poverty. Every Christmas the friend's mother told the children that Santa Claus could deliver only so many presents, which meant he could run out of presents, and if that happened, not every child would get one.

Of course, that little girl didn't get any presents. She further told my wife that she couldn't understand why Santa didn't start delivering presents at her house first, at least once.

I had much sadness to digest all in one day: the story from man from my office and the story my wife told me. Those stories caused my heart to bleed. I had no room for more sadness. How in the world does one fix some of these things? I realized that all I could do was to lend a sympathetic ear and I also knew that it was my responsibility to teach my children to be kind, caring and giving.

We should all strive to do that. Everyone benefits from giving. The problem is trying to sift through all the people who request our help to decide who needs our help the most and then determine how we should give it.

While I was in a town in Mexico recently with my family, we noticed people standing around every few feet looking for a handout. I am not overly willing to give to every person who asks because I don't always trust them. They might have a bank account larger than mine, even though they have chosen to beg on the streets.

My wife, on the other hand, feels differently. She pulled out some change and gave it to a supposedly poor lady. Our daughter decided that everyone who had their hand out should receive some money. Every few feet she would stand in front of her mother, fold her arms and tap her foot until the coins rolled out of my wife's pockets, and she would quickly drop them into a tin can.

Our son proceeded with a different method. He was carrying a few coins in his hand, and I noticed that he passed a lady who was holding her hand out for change. I asked him why he didn't give the lady any money, and he said without hesitation, "I don't think she's that poor."

Needless to say, his coins, all of them, made it all the way back home to America intact. Nobody was going to get his money!

Somewhere between what my son did and what my daughter did in Mexico is the right thing. I'm not exactly sure where the line is, but it's there somewhere.

We must give in this world, but we must give wisely. It is too bad there is not a rule book on life to tell us when, how much and to whom. That's up to us. I'm still working with my children, as well as myself, on the issue. I'm sure I'll have some hits and misses, but hopefully, the former will outweigh the latter.

I guess that goes along with the old saying, "You've got to keep on going on."

As long as I keep caring, I'll keep on giving. It's not up to me to solve the world's problems, and I'm glad, because I know I can't, but I also can't help but feel the sadness pouring out at me when I hear stories about poverty.

I'm not really sure how to end this, but since I heard a whip crack behind me, I know it's time to go. "Honey, where did you get that outfit?" (Just kidding).

SOS

It seems to me there must be an incredibly large waste basket for time and the events that come and go. If you have never listened to an older person and really lent them your ear, then you are missing out on much of life. In actuality, you are missing out on a gold mine. Everyone has a story to tell. If you don't take time to listen, you are definitely the loser. This story is about my Dad, who taught me a lesson on how important it is to listen to people.

It all came about when my brother and I decided to ask my Dad to allow us to film him while he told his life's story. Some of the stories he told were incredible. That was the first time I became aware of the fact that I only knew about a small part of his life.

After my brother and I had done this, I found myself telling everyone who would listen the stories I heard from my Dad. If I had been any more down to earth, I would have needed eight hearts and would have to fold up like an accordion in order to move. I'd also be in a great shape for fishing. Anyway, on with the story.

I received a patient in the ventilator unit who was a stroke victim. He appeared to be the type of person that one could have a beer with on occasion. I'm not sure how to translate that statement, but I felt it. He had the bushiest eyebrows of anyone I had ever seen. As he lay in bed he looked around the room as if to tell anyone who would listen that he was there among us even though he was unable to utter a word.

His left side was paralyzed, and speech was no longer possible. As a form of communication between us, I asked him to use his eyes or to squeeze my hand if he understood me. I'm a firm believer that if you've ever seen a stroke victim and not tried to communicate with him or her, it's not the victim's fault if you didn't have a conversation.

It didn't take me long to love this gentleman. On my rounds I would tell him what a good looking guy he was and when I did, he would turn his head to the side and open his eyes, slanting them at me. We joked with each other, in an unusual way, and I knew he loved the exchange.

When I talked to him, I always touched his forehead to let him know that I cared for him and about what happened to him. I wasn't there for the short term. I was there until his maker was ready to come for him and I was going to make sure he knew that I cared.

I knew he was a good man. He had worked hard all of his life and taken care of his family, day in and day out. He had met his obligation. He was a man where his word was truly his bond. I didn't have to hear him say any of this. I just knew it.

He had pictures of his family sitting all around him, because he loved and cared for them. About a year after I had been taking care of him, I saw a picture of him in his service uniform. As I looked at the picture, I thought of how he must have had the world by the tail at that time.

He had been a Navy man and that was especially dear to me, because I served my military time in the Navy as well. One of the pictures showed him bearing the insignia of a signal man on his arm. We had talked about this a number of times.

One day while I was making my rounds in the hospital, I joked with him about teaching me how to do the SOS signal. He lit up instantly, and his right hand started to signal. I almost gasped in surprise.

He took off waving and didn't seem to want to stop. It might not mean anything to anyone who is reading this, but, believe me, it sure made my day. Suddenly, all of the bad things that had occurred that day were erased. I was thrilled. The nurses, along with me, went off like rockets when they heard about it. It was great.

Every time I went to call on my Navy man, I would ask him for something. It would not always be the same thing, but it didn't matter what I asked him, he would always signal to me because he enjoyed this so much.

When there were other people in the room, they had no idea what he was doing, but it didn't matter. If they did, it would have taken away from the dream that no one else could touch. While signaling, this man was twenty years old again in the Navy, showing off his skills.

He died about a year later and I was saddened with his passing. I needed him as much as he needed me. A few weeks went by and I got up the nerve to ask his family if I could have that picture of him in his Navy uniform. A few more weeks went by, and much to my surprise, the picture arrived in the mail.

That man touched my life and every time I look at that picture I imagine what he must have been like back then when he was a Navy man. I'll have a beer now, and reminisce with thankfulness about the eyebrow man who came into my life and shared some time with me.

"Cheers to the only signal man I ever knew!"

I Hide My Hands

I loved him so much.
I know you did.
You don't understand.
I think I do.
I can't go on this way.
You have to.
No, I can't.
Does anything make you happy?
My children, they make me happy.
Well, you'll have to go on for them.
I know, but, sometimes I don't think I can.
Please don't do anything bad.
I won't, but, I can't go on like this.

I was grateful the day this lovely couple, who were both in their mid-eighties, came into my office, to be my patients. They acted like newly weds, the way they fussed over each other. It was just beautiful. I don't know what else to say.

The wife had weathered time a bit better than her husband had, which proved statistics once again. The husband had heart problems and he didn't survive very much longer, after procuring me as their physician. I had talked to his cardiologist and he expressed to me that he too, thought the two of them were a beautiful couple. Now, it was my turn to try to help this lady through a very difficult period in her life. This was definitely a challenge for me. It was like putting a broken glass fixture back together that had gone back through the phase of being sand. I also thought about the way I would feel if I was in those so called, "golden years" and my spouse had died. I would be lost too. I knew my words had to somehow help this lady to want to hang on. Every time she would come up with words of sorrow, I felt like a sweating boxer, who had been knocked down to the ground, trying desperately to recover. I had to help this lady. Dying of a broken heart is no way to die, because when that happens everyone suffers. Believe me, I had seen it before. I wondered about what I could do to help this lady and I also wondered about the dependency issues, here.

Sometimes, we overshadow our loved ones so much that they lose their self-reliance. I know if my wife died I would be totally lost, because there would be no one standing at the front door on Monday, handing me my five dollars for the week. Not to mention, when I get home on Fridays, her checking to see if I spent it. I'd not only be lost, I'd be devastated. Of course, this is all in jest, but, remember, truth lies in jest.

Now, I was being faced with having to dissect what parts were in play with this dear lady. First of all, I didn't want her to die of a broken heart. If she did, then the last thoughts she probably would have, would have been sad ones. Was I being selfish in my not wanting her to die this way? Was she using me as a sounding board, or, was she crying out for help? Was she being brave in front of her family and showing me the true side of things, now?

In order for me to help this lady, I had to dig into my soul and everywhere else I could think of. In order for me to be able to answer some of the questions that were haunting me, I had to assume that she did want my help, and sometimes ears are the strongest assets we have, so, I knew that I had to listen to this lady. When she would get off of the tracks, I would gently nudge her back on them. She talked and I listened. I had no idea whether she could even write a check on her own, but I do know that there are a lot of loving mates who can't write checks, or deal with any of the day to day mundane stuff that burdens us all. I did know that her family was not an issue, because they loved her very much. I'm also seasoned to the fact that some of my patients tell me things they wouldn't even tell their own families.

I've been seeing this lady for a few years now, and on each visit, I try to chip away at the negatives and accentuate the positives. The last time I saw her was earlier this week and she was a little more up, until I asked to see her hands, so I could check her pulse. She said, "I hide my hands!" She went on to tell me that she hides her hands, because they are now ugly and old, and this and that, and so forth and so on. Well, what was I going to say to her now? I had just finished reading a self help book about being grateful. I feel that self help books are a good way to aid each of us through a society that has complexities galore. Of course, complexities are injected here, instead of the end product of hay. That's not to say that I don't enjoy a little nitrogen in my life. It's just that some of it is a bit tart for my cerebral palate. Now back to the show.

After the lady told me that she hides her hands because they are ugly, I felt a strong need to try to make her feel better about herself and to help her to feel more positive, and I said, "You're beautiful. When you came from your mother's body, covered with goo, you were beautiful. When you dirtied your diapers, you were beautiful. When you went from a teenager to a woman, you were beautiful. When you were having children of your own and raising them, you were beautiful through it all. Now, look at your hands. The skin is thin, showing the veins that carry your blood through your beautiful body and soul. You are still able to feed and bathe yourself, so, you should not let a day go by, without being grateful for the beauty that you possess. Even if you couldn't do those things, if that ever happens, there would still be room to see beauty."

It's easy to miss the good things in life when we choose to harp on every negative that passes our way. This lady's family has now chosen me to be their physician, and I'm grateful to be their care giver.

Wolves in Sheep's Clothing

You must hurry up and get that out.
You must never be far behind the crowd,
It must be there when the customer wants it.
Nothing matters, except what pays.
Money is time and time is money.
You have to be better than the other guy.
You have to get rolling if you ever want to get
ahead in this world.
You always have to strive to be Number One.
Never turn your back on your competition.
Work, work, work, work, work.
Take a little time out for yourself.
Keep your emphasis on little.

A surgeon and I run a regional burn unit in a hospital. From time to time I tap into his expertise, which he has drawn from years of service to the community. In this capacity he is my mentor and a dear friend as well. He always seems to have the answers to questions on life that I feel I need to know. We both run a tight ship. Quality is our first priority, but we find time for doing the things we want and need to do.

When I first started out as a practicing physician in a fairly good-sized town, I got referrals from some of the local doctors and was very grateful for the confidence they showed in me. Some of them were truly in need of my expertise in internal medicine, while a few of them were just looking for a dumping ground where they could send patients they no longer wanted to deal with.

No matter how people may perceive the medical profession, it does have a business side to it. If a doctor works with his or her staff as a team, it runs along smoothly. Besides the importance of the doctor and staff relationship, there is a great necessity to be paid for services rendered because if the patients don't pay, the payroll cannot be met. It's as simple as that. Everyone who consumes at the health care table must pay a fair share of the price of the technology and expertise for which they have come.

Early in my practice, a doctor in the emergency room of one of the area's hospitals called me on occasion, seeking advice on how to care for a patient's needs. Then he would refer the patient to me. One day the person who handles my billing matters called my attention to the fact that nine of the patients who had been sent to me by that doctor had no insurance and so most likely would not be paying their bill.

I explained to her, "We doctors must take the good with the bad."

She said, "If we get much more of the bad, your practice is going to fold like an accordion."

I assured her that the doctor who had been referring patients to me and seeking my help, was doing his best to help me get started. I really didn't care because I was having so much fun being a doctor. All I wanted to do was to practice medicine.

I mentioned this to my surgeon friend, who quickly educated me. He told me that the doctor who had been referring patients to me was a partner with a doctor who worked with a large group of doctors in town. I decided to do a little research. I found out that the doctor was skimming the paying patients and sending them to his partner's practice under the guise of helping the new guy in town. Wow! He was actually out to destroy me, not to help me. Live and learn. I can be burned once. Yeah. But burn me twice? Never!

I quickly learned that not everybody who smiles in front of you is your friend or in any way has your best interest at heart.

So what was I able to do? I took appropriate action and dealt with it. Suffice it to leave it here. As the years rolled on, you can be sure I kept my eyes open for wolves in sheep's clothing.

My surgeon friend, whom I respect very much, has shared many a pearl with me with regard to the medical profession, people, friends, and other matters. We enjoy being with each other and talking about our practices. He is reaching the self-actualization phase of his life while I'm at the stage where I'm still grappling with which is the right way to put the toilet paper on the roll. From knowing this friend I've come to realize that we all need someone helpful and non-competitive to come into our lives. It makes things go so much smoother—rather like knowing there's always going to be cold milk when you're eating a peanut butter sandwich.

There Is Quality In Dying

We are constantly being amazed by the things that have come along in this century. We have found television to be a blessing as well as a curse. Years ago people were not living long enough to die of cancer. Then the antibiotic era was ushered in to save a lot of people's lives. By allowing them to live longer and take their higher chances as an older person, we led the way for them to be diagnosed with cancer. A blessing for many can be a curse for others.

In every hospital there is so much technology to be found that it can be frightening. Each of us as consumers of this technology have the privilege to pick and choose for ourselves. People will continue to get sick, and some of them may get well, but the bottom line is, no one lives forever. We will probably pay dearly for all of this technology. It is available and lies in wait for all of us. It is not for everyone.

If you are a smoker, for instance, you are living by a thread and will probably not be able to let your last wishes be known. Most likely, your decisions will be made for you. Smokers come into the hospital's emergency room unable to breathe. So the medical staff hurriedly puts them on a machine that will breathe for them. Sometimes breathing machines are good things to have around. The machine can help get someone out of heart failure for a few days, back on their medications, and then home. This is an appropriate use of modern technology.

However, if you have smoked yourself into a corner you will be sure to spend your days in a nursing home hooked up to a ventilator. For some people that would be a quality life, but for others it would be like living in a hell on earth. You must decide for yourself in order to save your family the anguish of making the decisions you should have made. You owe this to your family as well as to yourself.

I once met a man who was surrounded by the most loving family anyone could ever ask for. He was fairly healthy and had been fortunate enough to crack the code from within some years ago and stop smoking. Time went by and I continued to monitor his care and he did well, until a cough turned up a lung cancer. He was a surgical candidate and also received other forms of therapy, but he did not do well at all. Everyone, including himself, was in denial with the events as they turned up.

I tried desperately to explain the procedures to the family and prepare them for the end, but the man's sons kept directing me to look elsewhere because something was missing. Every lead had been chased down and the man's body had been scanned to the max, so I felt pretty sure that nothing was missing.

I digress. I am from the school of thought that no one can ever be one hundred percent sure that they are not missing something in their diagnosis, because if you ever get that comfortable with your diagnostic skills, you are sure to hurt someone. Never turn your back on any possibility, because as sure as you're born, you'll miss something. I always talk to the patient and try to be sure that they understand.

The man finally seemed to understand, and I felt good about this, but I still had a family on my hands that couldn't believe that their loved one was dying. They challenged me at every turn! I offered them names of every second opinion doctor that I had available in order to give them some peace of mind.

That's another school of thought I subscribe to. I offer my patients and their families the choice of getting second opinions, to let them know that I do not in any way know everything, and that I am very comfortable in getting outside help and advice. My ego is never a part of my day-to-day patient care.

I promised this man that I would keep him as comfortable as possible and said good-bye to him. He left the hospital to die at home, where he could be with his family.

When I think back on this particular situation, I wonder if his children missed a chance to say good-bye and to tell him that he was loved. I also wonder if anyone told him that they would follow up on his wishes and dreams, so they could carry them out the way he would have wanted them to.

Too many people die in a hospital and not at home. It used to be a ritual for the family to sit around at home and talk about the good old days, and this and that. They would do this while someone would be lying on his or her deathbed nearby. This ritual has all but become extinct, mostly because of technology. Our society has created this good monster, but somehow we have not worked out how to use it in the most appropriate fashion. It is good for doctors to do all they can to help their patients. It is not always good to do all that can be done. Either way, the patient must decide. We must educate ourselves so that the best decision can be made to fit each one of us.

Norma

I was prepared to handle your lung problem
today
Ready to go over your heart meds, as well.
My training has provided me with good
resources to help.
You were going to get your money's worth!
You've been a great patient.
We've had some pretty good visits.
You fuss at me. I fuss at you.
The common theme is, you won't quit smoking.
When you asked me what you asked, I was
unprepared.
Maybe I wasn't listening very well.
I get caught up in trying to think I can help
with most things.
When I found out today, I couldn't help as
much as I'd like to
I promised that I would give it some thought,
and I will.
I'll do the best I can!

One day one of my lady patients came into my office, needing me more than I thought. She had a problem I should have been aware of, but I somehow missed the boat. She came in for a routine visit and we fussed a little over her continued smoking. She heard my side of the story and I heard her side. She said, "I'm eighty-two years old. So what if I do smoke. Who cares?"

We went around and around, in our usual fashion, and then she got real serious with me. She said, "Can I ask you something?" I get a lot of questions from my patients. Most of the time they ask me how old I am, and how long have I been in practice. But that day she laid me out with a problem. She said, "I want you to find someone to live with me." That was it. No more joking around! That lady needed some real help here.

"I'm desperate," she said, "I'll even take a homeless person."

"But why are you so desperate?" I asked.

"Because I don't want to give up my house. I would rather die than give up my house," she answered. "All I need is for someone to help me a little around the house. Nothing big. I'm tired of reaching for things and falling."

I promised to try to help, but she had to give me time to think about her problem. I really wanted to help her. I thought that maybe I could come up with a good idea, but I needed time. At first I thought about how easy it would be to find someone who could move in with her and help. Then I thought about the reality of the situation. It was an impossible task to ask anyone to do.

A lot of what-ifs kept running through my head. What if a college student needed a rent-free atmosphere? What if there was another lonely person that needed the same help and companionship? What if there was a way to do some matchmaking? What if all I could find would be a homeless person? Would she really want a homeless person? Would she really want a perfect stranger? I'm sure she wouldn't want to share the same roof with someone who could be potentially dangerous! What if someone would move in with her and steal her blind? What if someone would kill her and leave her in the crawl space? This was not going to be easy.

I turned to a clergyman, a friend of mine, who I knew was a thinker. He seemed intrigued, and we parted, both agreeing to think about what we could possibly come up with in our think tanks.

Meanwhile, I have a lady who needs some help. I may never figure out in time how I can help her. But, if I'm unable to help her, I still feel an obligation to try to come up with some solution for anyone I might be able to help. I don't know the answer to this, but I would be happy to hear from anyone who would be willing to help me with this problem.

The Nature Of Things

I am so beside myself. I don't know what I'm
going to do.
What is it, Ma'am?
It's my son. His wife's leaving him.
I'm sorry.
She says she just doesn't want to be married
anymore.
How can you just one day up and say that?
Do they have children?
That's the worse part of all, they have two
beautiful children.
How could you turn your back on two
beautiful children?
(My head spun as I thought of ways I could
help her.)
I know you don't have time for this, but I have
to tell you something.
My husband, well, you know my husband.
He's so European, (whatever that means).
He says for me to just write them off,
but they're raising my grandchildren.
My son's my baby. How can I write them off?
I can't just write them off, you know?
They're caught up in some kind of a dream
world of material things. How can I help
them?

Dominick Acquaro, M.D.

I did a lot of listening that day. This lady needed to be heard. She had a truckload for me and I sat tight. There seemed to be a common theme as she went over the many reasons that things are the way they are. The message I kept hearing was that there aren't enough stay-at-home moms. What's happened to settling for enough?

She was my last patient of the day. I was thankful for that because I wasn't in any rush and could spend as much time with her as she needed to get off her chest what was troubling her. By the time she wound down, she was well spent, and so was I because I had ended another long day in my practice. As she was leaving my office, she gave me a hug and thanked me profusely for listening to her.

Before I left the office, I sat down at my desk and reflected on the day's events; my rounds at the hospital, the patients who had come to me for medical care, etc. That morning, I had been called into the hospital to see one of the burn patients, who was having some problems with his breathing machine. I had thrown all of my expertise into that crisis, until he finally settled down.

During the day I had made a few adjustments in blood pressure medications and had changed some insulin doses. Everything I had done was important and required a certain level of training. But the skill I had been trained in the least was to listen to a patient with family troubles. As I drove home I realized that sometimes just listening to a patient is the most important thing I can do. I felt it was important that day!

Gangrene Leg

It's gone too far. It already has you quite ill.
There are things that must be done, in order for
    you to get better.
You've got to be kidding, lady?
What kind of fool-hearted idea is that?
Listen, maybe you didn't hear me.
Oh, you heard me all right?
Listen, lady, you're surely going to die if I don't
    get a surgeon in here fast!
I don't understand. You're telling me that you
    came into this world as a whole person, and
    you want to go out the same way.
You are going to die.
This is gangrene, not a cold sore.
I don't think you're listening to me.
You know, you must be crazy, if you think I'm
    going to let you make a decision that is
    going to kill you for sure.
I know, you're seventy years old. I heard you
    already.
I know, it's your body. I know you have the
    right to decide.
Now, are you ready to listen to me?
You are going to die, if you do not let me get a
    surgeon in here, fast!

I know you want to go out a whole person. I've
heard everything you've said.
You're prepared to meet your Maker. I heard
you.
I heard all this, but will you please listen to me
for a change?

When I was in training, I kept up with my work load and studied very hard to be sure that when the day came for me to get my board certification out of the way that I would be ready to do my thing. After I passed the examination that gave me board certification in internal medicine, I knew I had made it and that I had finally come to the time in my profession where I could be the best that I could be. During my residency, the following happened.

It was a routine day for me. I got up around 4 a.m. and started my day reading. I read for three to four hours and then I went into my morning reports. This day my hospital duties brought me to a patient who had gotten into trouble with gangrene and the gangrene was spreading rapidly. The usual procedure for a resident in training was for the attending physician to walk into a patient's room with the resident following. If there were any medical students around, they would come into the room after the resident.

As I entered the room, the attending physician was telling the lady abruptly that her leg would have to come off. He wasted no words or time. He told her in such a way that we low-lifes thought we had surely found the long-awaited king of matter-of-fact. I'm sorry for my cynical approach to this, but, as he spoke, I watched the lady's face very carefully, and her expressions let me know under no terms that she would ever consent to have her leg cut off.

That's when things went sour. The lady was going to keep her leg and she had every right to do that, but the unfortunate thing was that she had been forced into a confrontation. There was only one person in that room who had the right to decide about this leg of hers and she held her ground!

There is an old saying, "You cannot win if you don't play." On the other side of that coin I have learned that you lose only if you argue with ignorance. This lady argued with ignorance and won. The physician standing in front of her in all of his glory had no idea that he was the one who was losing. I imagined myself jumping across the bed, grabbing the attending physician around the neck and giving him some well deserved nudges. With each stroke of my knuckles and with my mouth tensed just enough so that I could make my words come out just right, I heard myself saying, "You are not listening to her. What is the matter with you?"

I decided to stand there and try to think of some way I could better the situation. Nothing came to mind until the attending physician had gotten through with his temper tantrum. Everyone was pissed off to the high heavens. When everyone had exited the room, I thought about what was needed here. I also realized that the events that had taken place in that room had resulted in an education for us all. The lady was right, the attending physician was wrong, and something had to be done.

What I wanted to do was to punch the attending physician in the stomach and jerk him into reality, but I knew that wouldn't go over well. I suggested instead that we get a medical ethics consultant because it would help us all in our learning efforts. It seemed like a good day to teach the teacher, but I'm not sure the teacher was listening.

Could You Imagine?

Could you imagine?
I don't want to.
Yeah, but think about it.
Hey listen, I don't want to think about it.
It could happen.
I know.
What would you do?
I don't know.
Could you even imagine?
No, I can't even imagine.
She seems pretty strong.
Too strong.
I wonder...
Yeah, me too.

I consider myself a very fortunate man, and I'm not weighing any of this consideration on the word "fortune." I thank God that my family is alive and healthy. With each pregnancy there was great joy as well as the dark cloud of the "what-ifs." Sometimes the mere mention of the "what-ifs" would be quickly responded to and shot down to earth. In our house the "what-ifs" are ninety-nine point nine percent finished off with the phrase, "Don't even think about it." I'm not sure that's the right way to handle them, but it seems to work.

As an internist I'm surrounded with a lot of sadness every day, so I understand that we have to "what-if" on occasion. I view the peaceful death of a diseased person who has been in pain and suffered as a just reward for a long life.

I'm several years past middle age as I write this, and I've not yet experienced the loss of an immediate family member. I hate it when I lose a patient. It makes me a little crazy and turns me into a tailspin. If I'm lucky and live long enough, I know I will not escape having to deal with the sadness of losing a parent.

I have consistently made one observation, as if it were nature's law. No matter what happens, or how sick the patient is, the majority of people are not prepared. Is this because they didn't do their "what-ifs?" How many deaths must we go through? Is it like praying the rosary? Is it a ritual that we must not ignore as we gain the right of passage?

I don't know all of the mysteries that are tied to the "what-ifs" nor do I understand if becoming a "what-if" person would do me any good. Perhaps it could even destroy me. Who knows?

A few years after I began my medical practice, my wife met up with a "speak your minder," a person who spared nothing to let us know what she was thinking. As time passed, I began to like the person through my wife's conversations, and I hadn't even met her yet. It seemed like she knew the precise time of every one's colon checkout time, and yet she was not a nosy person. She told a lot of stories and was the type of person who says whatever hits her brain, at the moment. Her brain worked like rapid fire, which made it easy for words to roll right off of her tongue.

One of the most recent stories she told us was about her husband preparing diligently to put together a large group for a convention. He was going to be the keynote speaker, but he had given no thought to making a room reservation for himself. Well, you've guessed it, all of the rooms were sold out at the Convention Center Hotel. His wife called and threatened to move the entire group elsewhere, and "poof!" suddenly a room appeared for him.

She could probably convince Darwin to write an extra few chapters if he were alive and evolving with the rest of us today.

Some years back, this woman finished having her children. She had three small children, who were very close in age. Now, that's enough to take anyone out. Did I mention that she is a strong lady? In the midst of the joy she derived out of motherhood, she found out that her middle child, her only girl, had a blood cancer. I'm not sure if she had ever been a "what-ifer," but now she, along with her whole family, was forced to graduate to "What now?"

At first, when my wife told me the story about her new friend's little girl having cancer and about all of the tears and struggles they went through, I tried to ignore it. I didn't want to listen. I had two small children of my own to think about, and I hid from the "what-ifs" until I finally realized that I could learn something from this lady. Is that selfish? I don't know. Hey, there are a lot of sad things going on down the block. There's a lady at the car dealer struggling with all of her might to choose the right color for her new car. Now, that's sad, right?

Anyway, I've grown to appreciate this person and have been able to understand a lot of things, just by listening to her. To some she may come across as abrasive, and to some she may come across as an uncaring person, but to me she comes across as a compassionate, caring, strong lady. I thank God that her little girl is now alive and well and free of her terrible disease.

Some time ago I heard on the evening news about a young pilot who had been shot out of the air, yet managed to stay alive and out of enemy hands for six days or so before he was heroically rescued. He commented over and over about how important his training had been because it helped him through this terrible crisis. He was labeled a very important hero, and today he still is.

We can never be prepared to hear such devastating news about a child having cancer. That little girl is my new hero; there are no ifs, ands, or buts about it. Even though my little hero beat the odds, the "what ifs," still pop out from time to time, because they are embedded in our brains. I'm sure they will never leave this house, but when we start asking, "What if?" we continue to work at finishing it off with the phrase, "Don't even think about it."

Wealth

You must be a rich man.
Why yes, I am, very.
You must feel very fortunate?
Why yes, I do, very.
You've got a very busy practice.
Why yes, I do, very.
You must have a big house?
No, not really.
You must have a couple of new cars sitting in
your garage?
Nope, not really.
I'm sure you have a place at the lake.
Nope. Not at all.
You probably buy a new car every year, or so?
Nope.
Now wait, when was the last time you bought a
new car?
1973.
But, I don't understand. You said you were a
rich man.
I am. I'm rich with a healthy family, a few
friends, and a great staff to help me care
for my patients.
Well, you know what I meant?
Yeah.

Dominick Acquaro, M.D.

One of the best buys I ever had in a car was a used—and abused—1973 Oldsmobile 98. Now, if you've ever seen an Oldsmobile 98 coming down the road, you would think it was a building or a yacht. It was huge. I saw an ad for this car in the Des Moines, Iowa, paper when I was a medical student. The old MGB I had couldn't take the Iowa winters, and I was desperate.

When I saw the car, I found out that the ad I had read about the car being a little rough was an understatement. There was no easy entry into the car from any of the four doors. Rust was eating away at the car from the back on the left side of the rear door. It had certainly taken a hard hit. When I opened the driver's door, the seat looked like it had been in a fight with a Great Dane, and the dog had won. It looked miserable. It had been chewed up beyond recognition. The color of the car was yellow, with a vinyl top of no recognizable color at all.

The people selling the car had to get rid of it, and I'm not sure for what reason. They offered it for a chance in a lifetime price of two hundred and seventy five dollars, and my wife and I decided not to try to negotiate for a lower price, mostly because the heater was in good working order. After we paid the folks for the car, we bought a pizza and shared a meal with them. They provided the soft drinks and the warmth of their home, while we all enjoyed the fellowship and meal.

The car kept us warm and on the road for the next two years. I did all of the mechanical work on it, which was nothing major, fortunately. The car even transported my wife and all of our belongings from Iowa to Pennsylvania, and all the time, we felt we had it made in the shade.

The Oldsmobile 98 was still in running order when we found out that some friends of ours in Baltimore needed a car, so we gave it to them. I'm not sure whatever happened to that car, but from time to time, I think of it fondly. How could I call myself a rich man while I'm still carrying around memories of a car like that? It's just not possible!

Annie

When I saw Annie I thought about a time when she was very ill. I thought about how things could have turned out if I hadn't gone to the hospital to see her the night one of the members of her family called me. I knew I was going to see Annie the next morning, so I wasn't too concerned, but when I got the call to go and see her as soon as possible, I was wary, because I knew that things had gone bad.

I walked into the hospital room where she was lying and smelled the acetone from her breathing. I knew things had gone bad, and that it was time for me to rock and roll. Annie was not just sick; she was near death. Her acid system was too strong for her to keep up for much longer. I'm sure she recognized my nervousness and was aware of the urgency I showed in my actions as I quickly prepared to get things rolling. I believe she knew full well that things were bad, but her eyes showed me that somehow she really didn't care.

It would be four years later before I would learn how bad her condition really was. For the next four years I carried on with my business as usual while she kept her secret.

About seven on a Friday night four years ago I got a phone call and was told that a lady in the hospital was having some gall bladder problems and was asking for me to come to see her. I was also told that her sugar was a little high, but the lab results were not back yet. The voice on the other end of the phone line requested that I take a look at the lady the following morning, before her surgery. I hadn't been in town long and didn't have a full practice, so I decided not to wait until the next morning. I was more than willing to go to the hospital that evening to take a look at the lady, hoping that the lab results would be back by the time I arrived.

When I walked into her room, I could smell the fruity acetone was coming from her breath. Starting with that moment, I knew it was going to be a long night. The lady was very sick. The results of the lab tests showed me that her level of acidity would not long be compatible with life. I knew it was really time. Let the games begin. I was ready.

I made sure that everything that needed to be done was done. The insulin drips had been started as stat as stat could be, and she was having a difficult time responding to the treatment. After a few more days, about the time I thought it should be taking, she came around. After a relatively short stay in the hospital, the lady was discharged and sent home, with instructions for her to come to my office for a follow up visit as an outpatient. She came to my office just as she was instructed and I have continued to follow up on her condition since that time. She continues to use me as her primary care physician. She is a very spiritual lady and makes no bones about it. I have really never given it much thought about anything that I've done for her, because helping people is my job.

After a few months had gone by, every time the lady would come into my office for a follow up visit, she would thank me, over and over. When she started doing that, I got confused, because I didn't really know what to say. On her most recent office visit, she said her usual, "Thank you," and then continued to say, "I wasn't thankful for what you did then, but I am now, and I want you to know it."

I wondered what she meant by, "I wasn't thankful then," so I asked her and she said, "I wasn't thankful then, because I was not ready to go anywhere, but to hell when I died, and I was happy about that. Believe it or not, I was content thinking that I would be going to hell. But I've finally figured things out, and I've gotten my life back on track. I am now a saved person, and that is why I am thanking you for trying so hard to save my life."

That lady was really truly thankful for me. I had touched her life by doing everything I could to save her. That was such a great feeling. It was good to think it, but it was better to be told. All that time I never once thought that she was upset with me, while she was resolving some inner issues. But, that's what she was telling me, because that's what I heard.

Disability

There's a trough in the middle that's lying on its
side.
I believe it was full a while back.
I wish I could remember when, because I would
certainly tell you.
It lies there, kinda still.
Hey, I bet it was a great idea to have this
trough around.
I bet it helped a lot.
I just wonder what it was there for, or why it's
still there?
I see you have a problem with your hand.
You have quite a bit of difficulty, I'm sure.
How did that happen to you?
It just happened, eh?
I will try to see if it helps.
But, you must try something...you can't go
around without help.
It's my job to help you.
I'm here to help you.
I'll see you in a few weeks, OK?
"Hey, that's a pretty strong handshake," I
thought, as she left.
I don't know, if I hurt that bad, I don't think
my handshake would be quite so good.

But, that's me, not her.
She said, "Here are some forms for you to fill
out, Doctor."
I remember this person.
She wants access to that trough in the square.
She had a nice handshake.
You know, that is a public trough, but I must do
my job to protect it.
Able is able...
Will is will...
Right is right.
I can do what I'm able, and I will do what is
right.
If you're able, but not willing, to work?
There are others that are and do, and to them
my hat is off.
It's them I'm protecting; them and the trough.

Years ago I used to watch some of the documentaries about people who try to get one over on the government by seeking unfair public access. Those people must be few and far between, but unfortunately, they are very creative, as well as demanding and abundant in number. I'm certainly not one to deny someone appropriate assistance, because that is why it is available. I'm just against the ones that try to beat the system, who are not truly in need. After all, everyone can't be out of work.

I don't pretend to know the answers, but I do know when the wool is being tugged over my eyes. When my sight seems to be suddenly fuzzy, I try to protect myself and all the other taxpayers from those who could, but won't work.

When I was twelve years old I got a job stocking grocery shelves and pumping gas. Later I car hopped to get extra money. I saw my Dad struggle in order to give our family the things we needed, and we barely got by. He worked hard, so that my Mom could stay home and raise their children. I respect my Dad's work ethics, but I always knew that there wouldn't be enough money available for me to attend college when my time came.

Instead, there was the United States Navy, which was more than willing to sign me up and give me a chance to earn the money for my college education. When that money ran out, I was far enough into my education that I could see the light at the end of the tunnel, so I got loans. This is not a "poor me" story. No. This is an "if you want something, there is a good chance that if you are willing to put some effort toward achieving it, you will likely get it" story. There should be a lot more palms that are blistered than are sunburned.

Why Did I Ever Get Old?

Johnny lives in there, just by the door.
His food is a little softer, now.
Not like before.
He calls for his Mom.
He's willing and waiting.
Life by the door, is a bit degrading.
Miss Suzie, sits just off to the right.
She's prettier, when she's not in the light.
She's growing tired of the way things are
She wants to play and have a good time.
Maybe go to the park, and slide down the slide.
Or, tag you're it...now, go run and hide.
Johnny came over and grabbed her spoon.
He's always late. He's never soon.
Suzie's diaper is wet. Her pants are full, but
Johnny's in the corner shooting the bull.
She'll sit in the mess that she made for herself.
She longs for her porcelain that sits on the shelf.
Her food runs down the sides of her face, but
Johnny's in the corner, and he'd help, if he could.
He lives in there, just by the door.

That's his stomach, that's making the sounds
that go "roar."
There's pudding in his pants that used to be
clean.
The smell of the room is beginning to get
mean.
He cries for his mom, and thinks to himself
About his toys that were left on the shelf.
Johnny lives in there, just by the door where
it's cold,
And thinks to himself, "Why did I ever get
old?"

Everyone has their own horror stories when it comes to being in a nursing home. I ran a ventilator unit in a nursing home, where for various reasons, the patients had to be on life support equipment. Some of the patients were there because they had failed to make choices with regard to advance directives on how they would not want to exist should the unthinkable ever occur.

I have aging parents, and hopefully, they will do things a little differently when they are infirm, because we children are able to care for them. God forbid should anything such as a stroke ever happen to them. I owe it to them, because I am in the medical profession, to educate them about living wills, etc., so that when the time comes they will be able to make informed decisions about their health care.

The poem above, was from one of the times that I sat at a nurse's desk and observed the lives of the people who were in a nursing home. At the same time I prayed to God that I nor anyone I loved would end up in such a desperate situation. I also pray at times for world peace and for others. But at this particular time, I was being exceptionally selfish, and was only including my family and loved ones.

While I was still at the nursing home, I saw a man sitting off to himself, and I kept wondering what in the world could possibly be going through his head. Why in the world would anyone end up in a situation such as that? For the most part, all of the other patients seemed to be getting plenty of attention, but this man looked like he was in limbo, not noticing anything that was taking place around him. When people walked by him, he never seemed to notice they even existed. He stared off into nowhere and appeared not to grasp anything. I certainly would not want to end my days in that manner.

I saw a documentary once about how the Chinese respect and revere their old, and it made me think that we people who live in the Western world may be missing out on something.

I love to chat with my older patients when they come into my office because they teach me much about life. I have discovered that older people who are still fortunate enough to have their wits about them are great teachers of life. It is my belief that some of their families have not discovered their wisdom because they are too busy working at getting caught up in their "get ahead" games to listen.

I talk to my parents a lot so that I can learn from them. They have a wealth of knowledge. They went through the depression, as well as World War II and the Korean conflict. They both continue to enrich my life with their wisdom, and I am so thankful to have them.

A ninety-year-old woman patient told me once that they really did a good job in medical school teaching doctors how to care. After wrestling this old lady to the ground, I told her she had it all wrong. Well, I didn't really wrestle her to the ground, but I did tell her that medical school was good and hard, and that it was my parents who shared and continue to share with me the art of caring for others. I'll finish more of this between stories and poems yet to come, but for now, back to the man in the nursing home.

While I was leaving the nursing home that day, I bent over his chair on the way out of the door, smiled at him and asked him how he was doing. He twisted the corner of his mouth just enough for me to know that he was still in there, somewhere. From then on, part of my rounds at the nursing home was to say hello to that man and acknowledge his existence, even though I could not change anything.

Sara

The trees are blooming whilst the deer run
amuck.
How could we know there would be terrible
luck?
She started one day not seeming quite right.
And then she began an uphill fight.
At first we saw so many white coats. . .
I can't finish this poem, because it is too
painful.
I'm sitting here, staring at the screen of my
computer trying to get it finished, but it's
just not going to happen.

A number of years before Sara came to my office she had been diagnosed with a very bad disease called Lyme Disease, which is transmitted by a tick bite that sets off a living hell within the unfortunate person—at least for those that are not caught early enough. Sara was almost eighteen when I first saw her. She had been through many terrible hospitalizations and had not been able to walk for awhile. She had to learn just about everything all over again.

All of that didn't stop Sara from smiling. She had a smile that wouldn't quit. She was always in the best of spirits. The kid was as sick as anyone could imagine, but that didn't keep her from telling some pretty good jokes. She was always more worried about those around her than she was for herself.

When she came into my office for the first time, she was about two grades behind in school, because of her illness. I remember her telling me that she wanted very much to get well and stay well enough so that she could graduate from high school. That was a simple request.

Occasionally Sara would have violent tremors, and they would sometimes respond to the antibiotics that I would prescribe. At other times, the tremors would run their course and stop on their own. She smiled through it all. Pat, who works in my office, quickly became involved in Sara's care. We discussed many times how this kid was so strong and vibrant and always smiling. I'm glad Pat got involved.

Over the next few years, Sara was admitted into a hospital several times. Each time she came out of her crisis, but she continued to get behind in her school work. She had enough setbacks that I was sure she would be in her late twenties before she could graduate.

Then something strange happened. The phone calls stopped. Time kept ticking by slowly and Pat and I wondered if we should call her, but we thought for no good reason, that calling her might put a hex on her. We didn't hear from Sara, and we didn't hear from her Mom. That was really strange, not hearing from either one of them. This went on for months and Pat and I stubbornly stuck to our guns and didn't call Sara or her Mom. We even thought that they might be angry at us.

One day, soon after we had practically given up on ever hearing from Sara again, two invitations to her graduation came in the mail—one for me and one for Pat. Both of us felt like Sara was one of our own who was graduating. Hell, we didn't think it, we knew it. Sara was a loved one of our own. I was in, and I knew Pat was in. This kid had taught us many lessons of life, through her struggling. She was the smile behind the pain. Everyone in my office loved Sara.

Pat and I traveled to Sara's hometown to attend her graduation party. She lived two hours away from my office and the first thing I asked her when I arrived at her house was, "Why would you drive so far to see a Doctor?"

Of course she smiled, and her smile made everyone around her light up with happiness. It was just like the good old days. I was so glad to see that Sara was back among the healthy. We arrived at Sara's house in the early afternoon, so she decided to take me for a walk to show me some points of interest in her small town, and we fit in all that we could in forty-five minutes time. The whole time we walked, she kept that pretty smile on her face. She was in her twenty-first year of life and just graduating from high school with a smile on her face. She was now preparing to go off to college. Her plans were not to give up, but to keep plugging along. While Pat and I were driving back home from the graduation party, we talked a lot about the miracle child that was inside of Sara, and we both felt thankful to have been a part of her special day.

The next couple of weeks I slowly got back into my routine and didn't think much about Sara. You know the saying, "out of sight, out of mind."

That was me. I had no phone calls from Sara, or her Mom, so I felt quite comfortable with that, because I knew that if I had no phone calls, Sara was fine.

Then I got a phone call from her Mom. Sara had suffered a setback. I told her Mom to bring her over to my office as soon as possible. Sara was having tremors, but in the midst of all the pain, her face was covered with a huge smile, and jokes kept pouring out of her mouth as fast as she could tell them. As I examined her, I noticed a big Lyme tick on top of her head. It was telling me that he had Sara under his spell and he was ready to fight.

I put Sara back on antibiotics quickly and worked out for her to have some home nursing in her home town, and I got involved in her care by keeping in touch regularly with the home nurses. We were all in the fight together. It was hard to remember anything good that was happening with this bad stuff going on. This happened around mid to late June. Sara couldn't help but to wax and wane with her responses to treatment. I handled most of her care through phone calls and updates.

One Monday morning in August I got a panic call from one of Sara's nurses. She told me that Sara's blood counts were getting bad, so I had her rushed to a hospital in my own home town that same day. She arrived in the afternoon, and I admitted her into the ICU Unit. Well, guess what? Sara was smiling and joking and she was sicker than hell.

A few hours later, her lungs had filled up with fluid, so I had to put her on a machine to breathe for her. Over the next few days, everything in her body shut down. Her kidneys, her neurological system, everything. I couldn't believe that this could be happening to Sara. It was a grim situation, and every medical consultant I talked to about Sara's condition painted the same grim picture.

On Friday of that same week, about 10 a.m., I got a call from Sara's Mom. She asked me to stop everything we were doing and to let Sara go. I told her to hang on and that I would be at the hospital around noon to respect her wishes. Pat decided to go with me, and we didn't say a word to each other on our way to the hospital. When I walked into Sara's room I realized the hopelessness of the situation and comforted Sara's Mom, without any words coming from my mouth.

I waited on Sara's Mom to tell me when she was ready for me to do what I knew had to be done. Sara's Mom wept her good-byes to Sara and I held back all but the smallest tear you could imagine and while I was shutting off the machine, I also watched the weeping of a mother who was losing a child she had borne.

I had so many mixed emotions. Something happened to me that I can't even explain. I knew I had to go back to the office and finish my work day, so I left the hospital with Pat and headed back to the office, almost as if nothing happened. On the drive back to my office, Pat and I had the same speechless conversation we had on the way to the hospital.

When I returned to my office, I finished my day's work and headed home. My parents were at the house when I arrived home and while we were having dinner, all of a sudden the most ridiculous thought raced through my head. "Sara would never have dinner again," I thought. "Never!" I very carefully put my napkin over my eyes, and began to weep silently, hoping that no one would notice the tears that were dripping into my plate. I got up from my chair and left the table and went into the bathroom, where I hid for the next two and one-half hours, unable to stop crying. I literally thought I was going to cry for the rest of my life. The last time I had cried was when I was fifteen years old. This crying spell was the mother ship of tears.

I still think of Sara often, and every now and then Pat and I will talk about her sweet smile and her jokes, but then we quickly get back to work.

Everyone who knew Sara lost a loved one, and I'm sure the people who knew and loved Sara learned important lessons from her. I'm a much richer person, spiritually, from having known her and I'm thankful that she came my way!

My Task

Mrs. Jones, you see it's like this and like that.
Well, that's what you say, but I disagree.
It's not happening to you, it's happening to me.
I was just fine until I saw you.
I walked, talked, yelled and kicked, too.
But, you see Mr. Dr. the (your) treatment has failed.
And you say that you did the best you could do.
You know Mr. Dr., you know I might sue.
I felt fine until you ordered those tests.
You needed some more, so, I didn't protest.
I did everything you asked me to do.
Well, you know Mr. Dr., you know I might sue.
But, Mrs. Jones, you know that you're ill.
It's not a matter of taking a pill.
Your disease is a bad one and you must listen up.
We haven't much time...sure, I'll pass you your cup.
Are you listening to me? Be sure that you do!
Well, you know Mr. Dr., you know I might sue.
Diagnosing is my job, it's what I do best.

Because of your symptoms, I ordered those tests.
It's a serious matter, there's no room to joke.
It wasn't my fault that you chose to smoke.
You're weak and you're tired and you do need your sleep.
We'll talk in the morning, perhaps you'll feel better.
Sleep well, Mrs. Jones, try and rest through the night.
You've had a rough day. You've had a bad fright.
You know I can't sleep Dr., don't you?
Well, you know Mr. Dr., you know I might sue.
I know that you're angry. I know that you're sad.
You must be depressed, and you've got to be mad.
The years that have passed have flown by.
You thought you would quit each time you tried.
With each pack you smoked, you thought and you thought.
Not me...No how...I'll never get caught!

This story came about after having the uncomfortable task of having to tell Mrs. Jones that her years of smoking had finally caught up with her.

So many times patients have told me that they almost wish they had never come to see me because just days before they were living normal lives, enjoying themselves, and cancer was not a worry. In a way this sounds crazy, but every human should understand it. All of us do things that we hope will never catch up with us. (I'm guessing with the "all" part, because I suspect that most of us do something we regret.)

Mrs. Jones was obviously going through denial and anger simultaneously. Part of my job is to break through the denial phase just long enough to make sure the patient understands that they do indeed have a bad disease. At times this can be very difficult, but it is necessary in order for my patients to be able to make the life decisions that are facing them.

Unfortunately, with cancer sometimes a person doesn't have enough time to go through all of the phases. Although it's a part of life, the fact is that in some areas of medicine, we are far advanced, while in others, we continue to suffer growing pains.

I remember talking with a patient some years ago, and she asked me a lot of questions that there were no real answers to, because medicine is not yet, and may never be, that advanced. I am a Board Certified Internist and the more I read, the more I know that there is a ton of questions that I will never be able to answer.

Mrs. Jones had a lot of questions, too. And with her I was batting only fifty-fifty on some of the answers. When she asked me questions I couldn't answer, I was honest and told her quite frankly, "I don't know...I really don't know."

She told me that her other doctor never said he didn't know. He always answered her questions, each and every one of them.

In a flash, my brain formed the following statement for her. I said, "If you go to a doctor and he answers all of your questions, then you better run like hell and get another doctor, because in this day and age we cannot cure the common cold, and we are working like hell to cure some of the bad cancers that seem to be cropping up a little too much for my comfort zone. I can only tell you what I am trained to know. I practice between the lines of knowing what I know and knowing what I don't know, and when I get out of that comfort zone, it is my duty to tell everyone I treat."

The anger that patients feel when they are newly diagnosed is directed at times like a sawed-off shotgun with plenty of buckshot. As a physician I must remain understanding as I allow my patients to vent their anger. When someone is really laying into me it can be difficult, but I have learned to stand firm and interject in a helpful manner, every chance I get. When I do that I can do plenty of good in bad situations.

It was not my job to point out the fact that Mrs. Jones brought her illness onto herself (although I chose to insert this into the poem). Instead, it was my job to listen and to help her get through her crisis.

Sure, I get pissed off just like anyone else who has had a bad day. My bad days are the kind of days when someone decides that I look like a good target to defecate upon. I'm thankful that as of yet the cigars I used to inhale, haven't come back, to haunt me, at least at this writing.

I did feel bad for Mrs. Jones because it could have happened to me and I'm sorry it happened to her and I'm sorry that it is going to happen to many more. As a parent I hope my children never pick up a cigarette, a pipe, or a cigar.

As a human I hope that I never pick up another cigar, but as a physician I hope to reach my patients soon enough so that they will quit smoking safely and in time.

The code for quitting is within each smoker, and I can only hope my diagnosis is timely. Try and try again.

Leon

You gonna help me, man?
I'm gonna help you, man.
Mamma said you would.
Then I will.
Mamma says you a good man.
I'm here to help you.
How come this is happenin'?
I don't know, but we'll try to find out.
You gotta get me well, man.
I won't stop tryin' till I do.
You da man, Mamma said you da man.
Hey, how come I sick?
How come you don't know what's up with me
yet?
You gotta help me, man.
I'm tryin', I'm doing the best I can.
I'm gonna have to send you somewhere else,
because I can't figure it out here.
But you da man, Mamma said you da man.
I'm not da man, I'm only a man and I'm doing
the best I can.
I've exhausted everything here, but I'm not
coming up with anything. I'm sorry.
Hey, that's OK, you still da man.
I wish I was da man.
Hey listen, you take good care of yourself, OK?
Yeah man, I'll hang.

Hey, you're back. What did they find out?
I don't understand. Why can't I get you some help?
Am I gonna die?
I hope not, but I don't know.
But you da man.
Come on, that's a pretty heavy load to lay on me.
I know, but I'm countin' on you.
I'll do my best, but I'm not God and never said I was.
Hey, chill man. I know that. I just need you to hang out with me.
Promise me that you won't leave me.
That I can do. I'll see you everyday.
I'll stick with you until some smarter being comes into the room and figures out what the hell you got going on.
You know I love you, man.
I love you too and I love your mamma.
I know you do. She do, too.

I met Leon's Mom long before I had ever met Leon and enjoyed chatting with her each time I made my hospital calls. She had a good sense of humor and knew how to appreciate mine. She was a very hard working lady, somehow destined to hover just above the poverty line, even though all she spent her money on was for clothing and food for her family. I was glad to be able to meet her husband and always took the time to visit with him when he came to the hospital to bring his wife dinner, on occasion. He was a hard working man and very dedicated to his family.

The Catholic hospital on the south side of Chicago was run by a hard-core nun who didn't take lightly to pranks. Somehow I was able to sneak them in, usually in the middle of the night because the angle from the hall to the unit clerk's desk was perfectly designed for me to nail a water gun shot and duck down the stairwell without ever getting caught, although the nurses always seemed to know who it was who had terrorized the hospital at three in the morning. There weren't enough of my kind to share the blame.

When I met Leon, he was a nice looking nineteen-year-old. He looked too good to be sick. Although I was not on service duty to make hospital calls, his Mom asked me if I would take on his case and help in any way I could. I'm surprised that she asked me to care for Leon because of all the games and pranks she had witnessed, but somehow I had convinced her that I was a good enough doctor to take care of her son. I felt proud that she had asked me.

When I walked into Leon's room, I said, "Leon, my man, get out of that bed and let's go have a few beers while we try to figure out what's wrong with you."

He was lying there in a hospital bed, looking as healthy as any horse I had ever put money on. He looked, without a doubt, as healthy as I. We talked for a while so that I could get as much history as I thought would be pertinent and while we talked, Leon smiled the biggest smile, as if nothing could possible be wrong. We talked about what a great Mom he had and about how lucky he was to have such caring parents. Hey, I got no argument from Leon, the man, with regard to his parents. He was right with me on that one.

I always make it a point to see each of my patients and examine them before I ever look at their chart. That way I feel like I am truly in a position to give my best opinion on a diagnosis without being prejudiced by someone else's thoughts. I respect the fact that I am fully able to utilize my diagnostic skills without any outside interference.

I was confident that I could help Leon because I had asked all of the right questions, and it was now time for me to examine him. My job was going great and I knew I would soon be ready to tell his Mom that everything was going to be all right. When I examine a patient, I start with the head and end at the toes.

As I was examining Leon, I felt some terribly large glands that were absolutely too hard to turn out to mean anything good. His heart and lungs sounded great, but his belly was full of one hell of a large spleen. What the hell was I going to tell his Mom? I looked through his chart and saw lab reports that I had never seen before. His results were so abnormal that there was no way I was going to be able to explain them to his Mom.

I went back to Leon's room and confronted him with a million questions. I didn't do it because I had forgotten to ask them before. I knew he had been straight up with me and very direct with his answers. I just needed some more answers. When I talked with Leon and asked him some more questions, I was relieved because I knew everything was cool with him. He hadn't gotten himself sick by any fault of his own, that's for sure. I knew also that it was my job not to judge, but to seek out any pertinent data that I could obtain in order to help him. He was a clean man. Whatever jumped on Leon did it on its own.

The hematology and oncology teams got on board, and we scratched our heads and butts incessantly, but to no avail. Leon was losing the battle and we knew it. Finally, we had him transferred to the University Hospital were we all hoped and prayed that God would send someone into Leon's room and make him well.

A few months went by. Each time I went to the hospital to make my rounds, I avoided Leon's Mom like a plague. I felt like a failure because she had put so much faith in me and I couldn't help. All I could do was to scratch the same anatomical parts as everyone else. I secretly kept up with Leon's care through the university doctors. They were fascinated and stumped, because nothing showed up while everything continued to grow.

Finally, Leon was returned to his hometown hospital, with no more information than he'd had when he left. I told his Mom, before he returned, that I would still be available as a friend, but that I couldn't help. Her understanding surprised me, but I don't know why. Hell, no one else could figure out what was happening to Leon. Why would she think I could?

By the time Leon got back to his hometown hospital, his spleen was twice as large as it was when he left. Shortly after he got back I went to visit him at the hospital and he was in good spirits. I ordered some blood drawn from him and later that day the tests showed a markedly decreased platelet count that didn't jive at all with the ones that had been done just days earlier at the University Hospital. They showed that he was critical enough to bleed in the brain if nothing was done. The following morning I sat in on a consultation session, while the guys in charge decided that the only way out for Leon was for them to go after the spleen.

They ordered platelets, and when I told Leon what had been decided, he was really scared. He made me promise that I would stay in the room with him during his surgery to make sure that everything went OK.

I promised him that I would, and told him that I never promise anything that I would not be able to deliver.

Surgeons have a special way of running an operating room suite. They let everyone who is within earshot know who's in charge. The time had come and the surgeon said, "It's show time, boys and girls!"

The surgeon ordered ten units of platelets at the beginning of the operation and very soon after they began operating, things started going crazy. Leon's lungs filled up with fluid, so it was almost impossible to oxygenate him. Things were going too fast in the wrong direction. I thought Leon would surely be pissed when he found out that he was still the mother of a monstrous spleen. Hours later, Leon was holding his own in the ICU, but he was still on the ventilator.

I checked on Leon every day while he was in the hospital. Every morning when I left home to do my day's work I was pre-occupied with thoughts of Leon. I made my hospital calls before going to my office and always stopped in to see him. For the next two weeks when I visited Leon, I would stand by his bed and rub his forehead and tell him that I was there for him. I always told him that as soon as he got off of the ventilator, I would bring him something good to eat and I would tell him the full story about what had happened to him in the operating room, and why he still carried his spleen the way he did. He needed to know.

Leon was quite the man and hell, he was only twenty. He had his twentieth birthday while he was in the hospital. I took time to talk to his Mom every day, and I told her many times, "I don't know" and "I'm sorry." I told her more than once, "Your son will have a lot of stories to tell his friends when he gets out of this place, that's for sure." I also told her that I was going to take Leon out for his first beer as soon as he was better, and that we were going to live it up.

I was in. Hell, I was family. His Mom always pointed out the trays of food that were left untouched by the patients who had been discharged. She would say, "What a waste. No one ever calls and lets the kitchen know." She treated me like I was her kid. I had a lot of love for her and a whole lot of love for Leon, my brother man.

One morning when I was visiting the hospital, I was running late and hadn't done my morning reports, yet, so I quickly went to ICU to see Leon and noticed that his bed was empty. I found the nurse in charge because I needed to know where they had moved him, so I could stop by later, before leaving the hospital, to see him.

How stupid I was to assume that an empty bed only meant that Leon had been moved, instead of entertaining the fact that Leon could have died in the middle of the night while I was resting.

I've learned through the years that I wasn't stupid, just naive. Leon was the man, and he taught me a lot about life, as well as how to practice medicine a better way. Medical school taught me how to take care of my patients, my parents gave me a value system and a caring attitude, but Leon taught me how to hold on tight and fight to the end.

I went to Leon's funeral and hugged everyone in the family and cried with them and shared his loss. I think of Leon a lot and every time I go back to my training hospital I stop in to see his Mom and ask her, "How are things going?" Somehow we never talk about Leon, but he'll always be in my heart.

Helga

You've been where?
I've been there.
But, where is there?
There, that's where.
When were you there?
Then, was then.
But then is not now.
Tis' now and then.
You're here, now.
And now is not then.
But, now is then.
But, what is this?
This is that...that I got then.
But, when was then?
When I see this...then is now.
I have to live with this somehow.
I'm sorry is all that I can say.
A number on your arm is tattooed to stay.

When I first started my practice I had the luxury of time, which made it possible for me to find out about and enjoy every little detail that my patients would allow me to know about them. I'm sure each one of them could write a book, but I'm afraid the atrocities of the world that my generation reads about would shine through too vividly. Some of the most horrific days of this world are nestled in the people we pass on the street every day.

Helga appreciated my care more than I could have possibly imagined. She would hug me and kiss me on the cheek, before and after each visit. She was a strong lady with a weak heart. We talked about everything. She would tell me stories about growing up in Germany, and all about the war. Unfortunately, there was a number tattooed on her arm, which meant that she was in Germany during a very difficult time. She had seen and experienced things that, I'm sure, would kill the average made-in-the-shade now-generationer.

When we read reports about the torture that took place during World War II and try to comprehend the truth, we tend to think or want to believe that it somehow could not have been so bad. We all want to believe that this is a great world, and that things aren't bad at all. When I saw the number on this dear old lady's arm, it deeply saddened me. Somehow I felt as if I had been chosen to see this in order to appreciate all the good things I have now.

Helga died of heart failure, and she suffered a lot of pain, but while she suffered, she remained strong and passed her strength onto me while I was caring for her. She was a special person who touched my life. I will always cherish the day she came my way. Thank you, Helga.

I'm Really Sick

(Me As the Patient, When I Had The Flu For the First Time)

Honey, I'm sick.
Honey, I'm really sick.
I know. I'm not kidding.
This is not like before. I'm really sick.
I know I'm a big baby.
I know, I know, but I'm still sick.
The chills, the fever, my whole body aches.
I can't even stand the covers touching me.
What the hell is going on here?
Hey, I'm really sick!
Is this what sick is?
I'm sick.
I can't believe this.
I'm sick.
How did that happen?
Honey, I'm sick.
I know, but I'm really sick.
Is this how my patients suffer when they have
the flu?
No more Flo Schmoo...
No more Poo Poo the flu.
Now I'm caught in a stew with the flu.
I'm stuck in a rut on my butt.
I'm a different man, don't you see...
Now that it has happened to me!

Dominick Acquaro, M.D.

Years ago, when young doctors were doing their residency someone had the idea of having them go through some of the tests that they ordered without a thought for their patients. As a result of this, the residents thought long and hard before they ordered tests.

Sometimes certain tests are necessary, but even then it is better to have an empathic doctor who has been there and done that, saying that he, or she, understands just what the patient is going through. That is much better than to have to deal with a never-have-been-there sympathetic one.

My day came on a Sunday afternoon when everything was going great for me. I was enjoying my wife and rolling around on the living room floor playing with my two children, and all of sudden, for no good reason, I felt like someone had pulled the rug right out from under me. I was going downhill fast.

I started to have uncontrollable, teeth-rattling chills, accompanied with on-and-off fevers. My entire body ached. Something was very wrong, and going more wrong faster and faster. When I finally gave into my sickness and went to bed, I couldn't even stand the weight of the covers on me, not even a sheet. I thought, "Am I dying, or is this just the flu?"

Either way I could not believe my body was not under my control.

I don't want to beat this into the ground, but I now have a much better understanding of the flu. Thank goodness my episode only lasted one day. Before the flu got me I had cried, "Wolf!" at the slightest discomfort, because I'm a big baby when

I'm not feeling just right. Now that the flu had me under its spell, I had to convince my wife how sick I was, and I was really sick.

There have been other times when I've hollered, "Wolf!" because I wanted my wife to fuss over me, but this time I was too sick to even care. It is known in the underground that there are a lot of people out there like me, but I'm out of the closet by confessing this one. I'm sure that my two children will cry, "Wolf!" from time to time because they will want to be babied when they're feeling bad.

The problem is when we start doing that, each wolf calling has to be much more creative than the one before. I'm certainly up to the challenge.

Gimmicks

Hey, you're smoking too much.
And you there, I wouldn't sit down, you might
break the chair.
You know, between the two of you...
One's a chair breaker, the other an air taker.
And if you don't quit soon...
You'll both need an undertaker.

As I was leaving my residency program heading out into the real world, an experienced physician approached me with an idea. An enthusiastic, excited resident, I was getting overloaded with advice. It was almost impossible to believe some of ideas the more experienced doctors were sending me.

This particular physician came up with an idea that was the ultimate in preying on other peoples' misfortunes.

We as physicians, should be there to help people, but I have to admit, that I cannot argue the point, that when the misfortunes of others turn up on our doorsteps, we treat and cure whenever we can. A physician makes a living when someone else is down. It is a business.

Anyway, this physician told me about a diet program, and if I would market it right, it could be a big money maker. Contrary to what you might think, I was excited to be getting into the real world, so I could help stomp out disease. I was so excited that I was beside myself. There was no way that I was going to pick out a segment of patients and prey on them. That's what I thought I heard the man saying. I felt utterly ridiculous even thinking this way, so I, in a very respectful way, told him to "F....Off."

A few weeks later, I thought, "Was he right about any of this? Perhaps a doctor would go along with his idea, and, after all, someone has to take care of those overweight patients."

But again I realized how wrong it would be. It was just a gimmick, and I have problems with gimmicks, because they never really cure the patient. Gimmicks only result in repeat performances and plenty of money from someone's pocket. Is that good? For some people, gimmicks could result in a win/win situation, but for the majority of folks gimmicks result in a win/lose situation.

Let's look at blood pressure problems versus obesity. First, let me go over some of the medical facts that I know about high blood pressure. How smart are we in medicine today? Well, for the most part, we are pretty good at describing disease processes, but not so good at telling people why they have the disease. High blood pressure is a great example of that.

We do not know why the majority of people have high blood pressure. What we do know is that we have a cupboard full of medicines to treat it with.

Not every medicine works the same, nor do they work on everyone who has a blood pressure disorder. Now, are we preying upon people by hanging a shingle and telling them that we can treat and change? It's not the fault of the patients when all of a sudden they have a problem.

Obesity is usually the first visible sign of blood pressure problems. When I began my practice, I was a fairly fit fellow, physically, but within the first three years, I was tipping the scales at an extra gravitational force of thirty pounds beyond what I should weigh.

I graduated to a size thirty-six waist. Boy, did that send me off into orbit! It sent me every place you could possibly imagine. Every place, that is, except the gym. I had and still have no time for that. So you see, I would make a pretty good patient. Even though I do not think of myself as obese, I know that authors of some books I've read would have called my problem obese if I weighed twenty percent over what my height calls for.

I take the usual road traveled, here. I bitch and nothing changes. Sometimes I think I should bitch more, because if I did, maybe the extra weight would just jump off of my body and run like hell. Now, why should I not think that I am obese? It's because my patients are my marker. They tell me, "Hey, Doc! You look like you're putting on some weight."

Obviously, comments like that make me feel bad. I do have mixed emotions about my weight. Now that my weight has leveled off, no one says anything, and that makes me feel good. This, I think, better defines obesity because when people say nothing, they say everything.

I believe that obese people suffer more prejudice in our society than any other segment of our population. Is obesity their fault? I don't think anyone knows for sure, but they are always blamed for their problem.

Who's sympathetic to them? Listen to an obese person for a little while, and you will find that they are not always sympathetic to others with the same problem. So, really, it seems that no one is sympathetic to people who are obese. Do obese people suffer? You bet they do. They suffer from within and have to live a lifetime of struggle and pain.

What are some of the possible contributing factors of obesity? Childhood abuse could be one factor. It could be sexual, physical, mental, or any other kind of abuse. People who are obese may have been poorly educated with respect to nutrition. They could have been born with genes they have no control over.

The simple minded would probably say that people are obese because of low self-esteem, but that's only a result, not a cause. I say, "No" to that.

Let's stop here with these possible causes. What can be done about the problem of obesity? Everyone gets the same lecture about how to eat right as if they would have never thought of such a thing. "Hey, thank you for telling me that. I would have never thought of that one!"

No, it's more complicated than that. Shame begets shame. How many people talk about abuse? Not everyone who talks about abuse has been abused, but many who do not talk about it have been. Some people who happen to be obese because of a genetic makeup talk about being abused because it is an acceptable excuse. Some people who have been truly abused do not talk about it because it is too hard for them to deal with the product of obesity. Being ashamed of their bodies is not a coveted thing. It's hell on earth for those people. Some of them even welcome death to finally end their suffering.

Obesity is a real problem in our society and somehow it would be nice if the ones that are supposed to take care of it were able to do so. Not everyone has the same reason for being overweight, but it would sure be nice if the ones that need help could have ready access to it.

How do we solve the problem of obesity? I don't rightly know. I don't think it can be solved by building more fat farms and talking about nutrition until everyone is blue in the face. If we do that we would only be treating the condition and not diagnosing it properly. That is comparable to painting over a rusted car. If the underlying repairs that are needed are not done, the car will have to be frequently painted and repainted. Treatment is better handled, when it deals directly with the problem.

In this world it seems someone has a gimmick for just about anything you can imagine. Do you want to quit smoking? Then bring cash, but, hey, there are no guarantees. Do you want to lose weight? OK. We'll get the extra fat off, but there are no guarantees that it will stay off. Do you want to get rich quick? Just buy and resell real estate. Do you want to be healthier? Then take these herbs. Do you want to be stronger? Then just buy this exercise equipment. Do you want to be taller, shorter, nicer, live longer, etc? Then just take a pinch of this and a pinch of that, and give us a chunk of your cash, and your wish will be granted.

Whatever you want can be yours. How long will it be yours? Well, you realize of course, there are no guarantees. For me, medicine is not a gimmick and I will never treat it as such. The brain surgeon didn't train so that he could sit around hoping that someone would have a head injury while they are skiing so that he could be there to save their life.

As for myself, I strive hard to be the best doctor I can be. I want to offer the best care to my patients, and be there for them when they need me. I cannot help everyone with their problems, and when I can't I never hesitate to use the help of other doctors.

No matter what, I'll always be there to help the patients who choose to come to me for their medical needs. I don't always know how to answer a question of medicine, or how to be a successful business owner, or how to defend my medical practice when someone argues the point of preying upon the misfortune of others, and I'm the first to admit it. I do know that I certainly don't like to see medical gimmickry being done.

I like my patients and enjoy helping them and caring for them and that is what it is all about for me. No frills, no thrills, and certainly no gimmicks.

I Just Had To Do It

Don't even think about it.
Well, I am.
It will bite you.
I doubt it.
You're gonna be sorry.
Nope.
It'll haunt you.
Forget about it.
I'm telling you.
I'm not listening.
You better.
I'm not going to.
You'll see.
No, you'll see.
All right, already!

When I was in college, for some reason, I signed up for a 500 level Psychology of Women class. I really liked being the only one to represent my gender in that class, even though I knew it would mean trouble. From the very beginning, the looks I got from my classmates were micro cuts that I was certain would make a rooster turn into a hen. I was doomed from day one, because every day the women in the class would cut into me, until they would finally have me rolling helplessly away from my rightful owner of my senses.

The class turned out to be very interesting and I always looked forward to it so I could learn about my potential sparring partners. After I finished the class, I realized that the best way for me to go on with my life would be by pocketing the old saying, "What you don't know won't hurt you."

One of my fellow classmates had been enrolled in another course with me. She was a talker, and I had previously listened to some of her dating stories. I remember one particular story that she told me about her dating a prominent professional who gave her this and that. I wasn't a bit threatened by her comments, because she was some twenty years my senior.

Everyone in the class already had their fill of her stories, because out of a decade of eight tracks, she had a way of missing seven when she told them. I always thought it would be nice if I could get enough courage up to tell her to shut up, or to change the ridiculous channel she was stuck on, but, I never did, because it would have made me feel like crap and I would have beaten myself into the ground for the rest of my life.

One day it came to me that this class that I was enrolled in, prior to any tissue destruction from the evil micro cuts, had managed to pierce through me in the direction of my safety deposit box.

One of our assignments in this class was for each student to give a talk on—whatever. Well, I found my whatever. The devil made me do it, and I did it, from vine to vine. I chose to talk about how parents hold their daughters back and about the encouragement daughters need in order to maintain dependency. I went through all of the stages of development and fattened the whole talk up so I could get to the end as soon as possible, because the end was what I really wanted the ladies in the class to hear. The end was that, women are like monkeys on a vine and they must have a good hold on the parent vine so that when their mate comes along, they will be prepared and ready to let go of the parent vine. That is, if they ever do let go.

I went on to fit in the talkative lady in my speech, in a way whereby, I was certain that she would feel the pea under the mattress and not quite know that it was there. Clever, probably not. Cruel? Yep. Funny? Not to those women. Successful? Yep, I got an A. I had no right to do that, but I did it, and it's over now. What did I get out of all of this? At the time, I got a lot of laughter when I told my buddies, and after a time I realized that my speech wasn't too far off base.

Many times when we hear a sad story, we know that there is a lot of truth within. It is the same way with humor. If there is truth built within a humorous story, it sounds funnier. The stories that hit home hurt people or make them laugh.

As I reflected on what I had done, I tried to search out, why, and what I could possibly take from my actions. I think the way I acted could be summed up on a maturity scale as being a bit offset, and I didn't derive anything good or bad from the experience. It is now only an incident out of my past that I can carry around with me and pull it out of my head when I want a good chuckle.

I've had women around me all of my life. My mother is a woman, my sisters are women, my wife is a woman, and my daughters will become women. To accommodate the women in my life it has been necessary for me to switch my way of thinking into a listening mode. Many of my women patients make me believe and understand that there are a lot of men who are stuck in the denigrating mode and the only way they can survive is in knowing how to play the game.

Some of the illnesses of these women are attempts to become self-empowered, to have some control. When I hear those stories, they aren't at all pleasant, and the faces of the story tellers aren't pleasant to look at, either. Their stories are sad and full of emotional trauma. The women who tell me such stories are going through sad times.

Often they have stuck it out for the man they love, or think they love. I don't know the answer here. Maybe it's too much vitamin T, or maybe it's just meanness. It's some kind of an epidemic, whatever it is. Men need to be taught never to forget that their wives are mothers and that their daughters may be mothers one day. When I watch sports on television, I see sports figures, thanking their mothers. Then, I see and hear about, an occasional sports figure mistreating a potential mother. Where do you draw the line?

In my profession, I hear about a lot of problems, and not occasionally; I hear them every day. Sometimes I will hear a different version of the same story on the same day. I remember hearing a saying one time, "Always treat your wife the way you would want the mother of your children treated." Men need to treat their wives with dignity and respect. They need to treat their wives with love because a wife is the queen of her husband's life, and she deserves it. Men need to teach their sons the same lesson on how to treat their wives. There should be no double standards, just respect.

Even though I work a twelve-hour day, I could never match the twenty-four hour day that it takes to be a good mother. It's a little past six in the morning, and it's time for me to take my wife a hot cup of coffee, because it will help her to start her twenty-four hour shift.

It's My Turn

A few years ago my Dad had a treadmill test that revealed some trouble with his heart, but he didn't want to have a heart catheterization to follow-up. We sat down out by my work shed and talked about the procedure. All he kept telling me was that he had lived a long life, seventy-six years, and was ready to face whatever would happen to him. I presented him with all the risks, etc., and when it came down to the possibility of his having to have surgery, it pretty much clinched his decision not to do anything.

Dad was a good Catholic and had put his fate and faith in the hands of God, and that was all he felt was necessary. I explained to him that the worse case scenario would be to have a heart attack and spend his last days on earth in heart failure, finding it very difficult to breathe. I told him he would be better off to die of a massive heart attack than to be left with no quality of life. He still held fast to his decision.

The burden weighed heavy on me because I had to hide my knowledge from the rest of the family. I knew at any moment I might get a call from home with bad news. All I could do was to keep busy and force the bad thoughts from my head every time they chose to enter. A few months ago, my friend's father got a wake-up call and found out that he had coronary heart disease, and I didn't tell my dad, because I knew nothing good would come from his knowing.

Dad would mention his heart condition from time to time, just out of curiosity because he had so much respect for himself. Then my sister's father-in-law had a severe heart attack, and he was left in the state that I had earlier described to Dad. Soon after, I got a phone call from Dad.

Now Dad was afraid, but he wanted no one to know of his fears. He called me and asked me in a matter of fact way what he should do about his heart problem. He was ready to pursue the medical help he needed. He was ready to take the risk that he was not willing to take two years before.

I asked a cardiologist to please take a look at my Dad to see how he was doing. When my Dad went to the cardiologist's office for his appointment, he explained his symptoms and my mother said that it was all she could do to keep her chin from rubbing raw on the floor. My Dad had been hiding his symptoms from me, from Mom, from everyone, and he was good at it. Time was getting down to the wire and his fear was taking over. He could no longer hide his symptoms or his feelings of fear.

The cardiologist scheduled Dad for heart catheterization, and the results showed him to have marked coronary artery disease. His pump had not been compromised but was a sitting duck for a heart attack. On Friday, my sister called telling me Dad's cardiologist had sent him by ambulance to a larger hospital many miles away. Since we work together, we discussed it and decided to leave right after work. When we had finished the day's work, we headed for our respective homes and quickly packed our bags.

When my sister arrived at my house, we put our bags in the car along with my family, and off we drove. It was a long trip, and we stayed overnight in a roadside inn. We finished our trip the next day and arrived at the hospital around two o'clock in the afternoon. When we walked into the room, the rest of the family was there.

We had a nice visit with Dad. The anxiety in the room was enough to fill a psych ward. Dad looked good, and I couldn't imagine how I could do without my father if things went wrong. I knew that the vast majority of patients who undergo heart surgery come out of it as if nothing had happened, but I was still scared. I could remember only the cases that had turned sour. Even when all of the skills are in the right place, something can always go wrong, and I couldn't get those thoughts out of my head.

A few days later, Dad was rolled out of his room into the holding area. He was very sedated from all of the pre-op medications. The doctors were kind and understanding and allowed me to spend the full hour before surgery with him, even though he was very groggy.

I kept my eye on Dad while I visualized the football he used to throw at me, how it seemed it would never come back to earth once it left his hand. I talked to him about the time he and I had decided to race at the ice skating rink. Instead of going in the direction of the oval rink, we decided to go straight down the middle. We were ready for a good race, and by the time we both got to the other end of the rink, we figured out that we hadn't planned our race very well. We hadn't planned for Dad to go right and for me to go left.

It sounds dumb now, and it was then, but we were caught up in enjoying the race so much that we ended up crashing into each other. We had a good laugh over this, and while I talked I rubbed Dad's head and told him how much I loved him and appreciated him.

Dad's surgery went smoothly, and even though he had a rough recuperating period, he got along well. He hates to rely on medications. A few weeks after his surgery, I asked him if he would do it again, and all he said was, "I think your question is a little premature, but I'll get back to you on that one, son."

The experience I had with my Dad's illness did not change the way that I practice because even before then I had always been helpful with my patients and their families, but it did help me to understand the process more.

My Wild Irish Rose

Day in and day out the machine goes
psshhh...ching
How did I get in the mess I'm in?
I'm tired all the time and it's so hard to eat.
I can't even talk with one breath.
I joked when I smoked, as I toked each toke.
I was sure my health would always be around.
But, psshhh...ching.
It's a terrible thing when your life depends on
that sound.

An extremely thin black lady with two lifetimes of woes behind her eyes was one of my first patients in the ventilator unit. She had literally smoked herself into a corner and had no chance of ever taking another breath on her own. When I first saw her in my office I told her that I would take good care of her, and she looked at me with continuous eye contact, until she believed I really meant it. She was the kind of lady who could bitch to the high heavens, and get just about everything she wanted.

The first year I was her doctor she came into my office depressed because her birthday was coming up, and she had no family that could celebrate it with her. Her first name was a typical Irish name, so, I affectionately called her, "My Wild

Irish Rose." From time to time, with the help of who knows who, she would dye her hair as red as red could be. I always gave her hell about this and we would have fun with it for a while. That was one way that I could keep her mind off of the fact that she was ill. I teased her a lot, but, more often than not, she would catch me in her trap, and I would be unable to get ahead of her on any subject.

To make a long story short, I went by the local grocery store and had a cake made with the words, "To My Wild Irish Rose," and I presented the cake to her on her birthday. In the middle of all of this, she managed to thank me and of course, get some bitching in about the way she was treated by my staff. It was a normal day.

My Wild Irish Rose got sicker and died a few years later, but she left me with a lot of neat memories and a picture of the cake I got her for her birthday.

Miss Rowdy's the Nurse for Me

The ICU nurse was really tough.
They called her, "Miss Rowdy." No one could
pull her bluff.
Some of the patients didn't think she cared
But she was not bad at being fair.
She cared for her patients with gusto.
I don't know why she had to fuss so.
That ICU nurse was the best I knew
Because she always told it true.
If I had to pick a nurse for me,
"Miss Rowdy" is the nurse that it would be.

Miss Rowdy was a dedicated nurse who threatened to throw her patients out the window. When I was growing up, Vietnam was a blazing story that appeared every evening on the news. A lot of young men from my home town found themselves in Vietnam, and many of them never found their way back home. It was sad, but because I was busy growing up, I never fully understood about the Vietnam War.

When a friend of my sister returned from Vietnam he referred to the enemy as "gooks," and he would tell stories about blowing the sh-- out of them. I knew they used the term "gooks" because it made it easier to describe someone they had destroyed.

Later I learned in college that in order to make everything all right in a war zone, participants need to dehumanize the enemy. They do this by labeling them with a fabricated name. This makes it easier to kill people in battle, people they believe do not deserve to live. It was an easy way to cope. This is the lead into a story I am not sure will translate the way I want it to, but here goes. . .

Part of my training as a doctor was spending time in ICU. At my training hospital there was a particular nurse we labeled "the nurse from hell" and "Miss Rowdy."

She said things that were completely out of line about the patients, and it would take days to get the goosebumps down that her talk would bring out in our bodies. On one occasion she said, "If I could open the window I would dump that man's can right out into the street." I hope the patient or any of his family never heard that comment. If they did, horror stories of nurses doing mercy killings on the side probably cropped up in their minds. But wait. . .

I watched "Miss Rowdy" because I was curious to see how she handled her patients. I was surprised to see how much she cared for them. She treated them like most people would treat members of their own family. When anyone crashed, she was the best thing going. No other nurse took up for the patients with such overwhelming loyalty.

When it came time to do something for a patient, “Miss Rowdy” was always there. She was the first to cry, even if it was in a subtle way, when she lost a patient.

“Miss Rowdy” had trouble coping with her emotions because she would get so involved with her patients’ problems. I don’t know if it was just an act or real, but she displayed her emotions for everyone to see, hoping they would buy it, and maybe hoping she would buy it, too. She was tough, no doubt about that, but she was also a dedicated nurse.

I hope this translates well, because if I were sick in the hospital, “Miss Rowdy” would be the first nurse I would choose to care for me.

The Ninety-Year-Old Sisters Who Watched TV and Never Talked

Two sisters who were ninety years old came into my office one day as new patients. Neither of them had been married. They never shared that with me, probably because I was never quite sure how to ask. They were both quiet but could be easily aroused into a joking situation. For some reason, when they first started coming to my office, everything seemed fine, and I joked and laughed with them, talking about everything under the sun to make them feel at ease. I enjoyed taking care of them, and I hope they felt the same way about me.

One day when the sisters were in for an appointment, I had a little time on my hands, so I asked them about their everyday routine. I said to them, "I guess that your day includes sitting around, talking about old times, and anything else imaginable, right?"

As soon as I finished, they paused as if I had asked them if they were pregnant or something. They looked at each other, and then they both returned their gazes to me, and said, practically at the same time, "We never sit around and talk. We just watch TV all day long, and then we go to bed."

Naturally, I thought they were joking, but I found out that they were not. I thought, "How could this be? How could two sisters not sit around and talk about all of the rich years of their life, and the things they had experienced and seen?"

Hell! Television hadn't even been invented until some years after they were born. So, how come they acted surprised with my question? I thought it was a fair one. Had I been thinking right here? Maybe I was talking too much. I know it was none of my business what the sisters did during the day, but I was curious just the same.

One of the sisters got very sick from a bad infection, so I admitted her into the hospital. Her infection was overwhelming, and I didn't think she could possibly survive. All I could think about was how she had lost the opportunity to catch up on the good old days by talking about them.

Again, I knew it was really none of my business, but I often think about the sisters and I try to limit my TV time in my own house so that I can be sure to give my family their quality, "talk it out" time.

I'm thankful that my parents set aside every Thursday night for our family to all meet together and talk. On Thursday nights we learned to communicate in such a way that we could get through the struggles that accompany growing up. It was important for me to have had this special time to share with my family when I was growing up, and it is important now, for me to do the same thing with my family.

Burn Patients Want To Survive

Could you?
I couldn't.
Would you?
I wouldn't.
I wonder if they'll hate us for this?
I don't know.
Would you?
I'm not sure.
Would you?
It depends.
Depends on what?
On how bad it is, that's what.
How bad is bad?
You know, bad!
I don't know.
You know!
What if they do hate us, what then?
I don't know.
Well, we would have done all of this for
  nothing, while all the time, thinking we
  were helping.
At that very point in time, someone hates us for
  what we've done.
Is that right?
I don't know.

I guess we'll never know.
I hope we never know.
I know.
I know you know.
You know you never can tell who'll thank you and who won't.
Yeah, but most do. Only a few don't, that's really why we do what we do here.
Yeah...I guess you're right.

When I first started my medical practice, I was excited about being involved with helping people who were in critical care, as well as being active in a primary care practice. In the town where I started my practice, it was almost impossible to crack the code in order for me to be able to be involved in critical care in a hospital.

Then along came Bob. He was affectionately known as "R.J." to everyone. R.J. ran the burn center in a hospital that was available to quite a large radius of people in the State of Indiana. He gave me a chance to work with him in this center, and since that time our team has restored some very ill patients back home with their families. We are a dedicated team. There are no weak links in our chain.

I'm not sure if it's a way to cope, or heal, but I always find myself wondering whether patients will be angry or grateful, when they are dismissed from the burn center, because they do not always leave in the best of circumstances. Some of them leave having to depend on dialysis, some of them without as many digits on their hands as they had before, and some of them leave with scars galore, but the most remarkable thing they leave with is an apparent new lease on life, even though they may leave scarred and mangled.

Most of them are thankful to be alive. I know they must question how they could be thankful when they first leave the hospital. They usually feel a little rocky at first because they know their condition could go either way. Everyone on the burn team is thankful when someone walks out of the hospital alive and can once again put their feet under their own dinner table. Thank God for the spirit and drive of life.

That's Easy For You to Say

Every time a patient who is a smoker comes to me, we talk about the obvious. I tell him or her, "you know you must quit this nasty habit."

Invariably the smoker will respond with, "Hey Doc, that's easy for you to say. You don't smoke, so you have no idea how hard it is to stop."

Now, it's my time for confession.

When I was nine years old my best friend was only eight, and one day the two of us were watching some army maneuvers being performed around the countryside where we grew up. While we were there we found a pack of cigarettes. We went to the nearest store, bought some matches, and contemplated what we were going to do with those cigarettes.

As we walked through the back roads, we found a perfect spot where nobody would ever see us and would not know that we had been there. There was an old church on the property, surrounded by a graveyard and plenty of woods. The road was far enough away that no one could possibly see us.

We each picked out a tombstone to stand by, and then we lit up. We had no idea how to smoke a cigarette, but, one thing for sure, we were going to give it a try. Even though we didn't inhale our cigarette, we got very sick.

I didn't try to smoke another cigarette until I was thirteen, and that time I had a lot of friends who saw me doing it. By the time I turned fifteen, I hung out with my friends at a local cafe every chance I got. It was the same cafe where I worked part time as a carhop, so I knew most of the kids who hung out there. There was a room in the back of the cafe where the guys would frequently come to play pool, and one day I saw one of my classmates standing by a pool table, smoking a cigarette, so I went over to smoke with him. That's when I learned that I hadn't been smoking right. He told me that I wasn't inhaling, and he was kind enough to show me how to do it. Now, as I look back, I realize that it was stupid of me to give him permission to influence me, because after that incident, I became a real smoker. My coughing and spinning head continuously reminded me of that.

Now on to fast forward. In 1982 I smoked my last cigarette. So now it is easier to tell my patients to quit. I tell them, "You can quit if you really want to. It is a code from within all of us. Everyone who smokes owes it to himself, or herself, to seek the code and crack it. There is never a wrong time to quit smoking. If at first you don't succeed, then try, try, again. Don't put the burden upon your spouse or someone else to take the responsibility of quitting for you. Take on the responsibility yourself, and when you do, stay a quitter. Remember, the urge to smoke will go away. You have to give it time. However, if you continue to smoke, there will be plenty of guilt for you to deal with. Did I mention that I'm a Catholic?"

What You See is What You Get

When I was in the second grade I got a part in my class play that may not have been the most coveted role, but the entire class encouraged me to take the part. When I was at home with the family, I never shut up, but when I was in school, I never made a sound. No one ever knew I was there. Shy was an understatement.

I remember the teacher explaining the parts and when she did, everyone screamed out the parts that they wanted. One of the characters in the play was a hobo who had to walk on the stage and not say a word. That was my part.

After I finished the second grade I decided it was time to talk and mingle with the crowd. I haven't shut up since. Certain situations still bring back that shy kid, but for the most part, anyone who knows me now wouldn't believe any of this.

While I was going through my residency, I would talk to everyone. It didn't matter if they worked in the boiler room or if they were the top executive of the hospital. When I had questions about old cars, I would talk to the man in the boiler room because he was an old car buff. We spent hours talking about old cars. It was never a big thing with me what title a person had.

Early on in my practice I noticed that people acted like it was a big deal when they were on a first-name basis with me. I never urged anyone to call me "doctor." That's not to say that I play down my role or my responsibility to my profession, but I don't want it to separate me from anyone.

While I was in my residency, I was required to wear a white coat and to introduce myself as "Doctor." I decided that my agenda outside the residency was for me to be an independent practitioner, and I chose to do it my way. My way now is to wear blue jeans, docksiders, no socks, and introduce myself using my first name. However, for certain age groups, I still address them as Mr. and Mrs. unless they ask me to do otherwise.

What good can come out of me dressing this way and using my title as a flotation device? Well, I have found that a lot of good can come out of doing it my way. I have discovered that when I do it my way, the time is cut down considerably when it comes to getting my patients to open up to me and tell me what I need to know in order to help them. Otherwise, it would probably take many visits before that would happen.

A casual appearance also takes a lot of anxiety away from the patients when they are in my office, which seems to work extremely well for all of us. I think it is the ultimate win-win situation. Does it work for everybody? No. The majority of my patients open up right away, as if we were sitting by a campfire chatting. When that happens, I feel great, as well as honored because they are allowing me to help them and are accepting me for the way I am.

I am not on a mission to change the world. I am explaining what happens to me when I do it my way, choosing to work in my own small corner.

Do You Not Realize?

She's a good kid.
How do you feel?
It's my stomach.
She does well in school.
How long has this been going on?
She has a lot of friends.
Is there any particular time of day when it
bothers you?
She's good to her brother.
Are you sick today?
She's my pride and joy.
Anyone else at home feel the same?

Well, you see, there is only little Nick, myself, and Lena here. John took off to God-knows-where and God-knows-why. It was as if he just didn't care about any of us. He just took off without taking any responsibility for his kids. He is such a loser. He sends a check when he damn well feels like it, and never comes around to see his kids. I make damn sure that I screw up his weekends with the kids, if he hasn't paid what he owes.

Don't you think that I'm going to let him get away with anything like that! No, not me. My Mom certainly did not raise a fool. Why couldn't

John have been more of a family man, like my Dad? Now you see, my baby is hurting. Well, do you think John cares? He doesn't, and he won't do anything, either!

He's causing all of this mess, but you don't see him here to pick up the pieces, do you? He's always claiming that I talk him down in front of the kids, but I don't. I wouldn't give him the pleasure of laying any blame on me. My parents really pound on him, and I don't even try to stop them, 'cause you know, that's not like me. We all have the right to slam him. I tell you, I get so disgusted with that low-down S.O.B.

Well, I think I know what your problem is.

That's great Doc, and you didn't even have to run any tests. Didn't I tell you he was good, Lena? Now what's wrong with my fifteen-year-old princess?

I. WHO GOT DIVORCED?

The mother and father should have been the only ones. However, they have conveniently included the children in their games. This parent, and many others, have not a clue as to the damage that is done to the children when they get a divorce. It should specifically say in the divorce papers, and be underlined, that it is the parents and not the children, who are divorcing. Even though I've used the mother and daughter here, it would be just as common if the father and child were in the room. Fathers don't seem to have control of their tongue when it is needed, either.

2. WHY DID THEY GET DIVORCED?

I'm not sure that the reason matters for anything other than to fuel one of the parents' insatiable appetite to get revenge. If you know anything about revenge, you know it is just for that reason, an insatiable appetite for getting even.

3. WHAT IS THE EQUATION FOR SUPPORTING THE CHILD?

X+Y=x+y
Now, X-Y still = x+y and even Y-X=x+y

If you made the child, it is your responsibility to support him or her. Usually, support payments are fair. A fair equation should include the needs of the child and not the needs of a vindictive parent. There should be an equation that would fit here so that the non-custody parent pays for the needs of the child. I don't know the answer, but I do know what belongs in the equation and what does not.

4. WHO IS EMOTIONALLY RESPONSIBLE?

X+Y, as well as both sets of XX's and YY's are responsible. That means everybody. If X's YY talks bad about his ex-Y, well, it certainly cannot be X's fault, if it is done in front of x+y. As a matter of fact, if you are not the bearer of the sword yet allow it to penetrate the soul of a child, then you, my friend, are responsible for the damage. It is your responsibility, whether you are the X or the Y, to protect your little x's and y's. The quicker you learn to drop the sword and disarm those around you, the better off x and y will be. They will have a chance to grow and grow and grow. Please let them grow!

Staying on Time

As my practice matured, I fell into a time trap. When I'm invited somewhere for a social gathering, I don't just arrive on time, I arrive early. When people give me a time for a party, or dinner, I respect their request enough not to be late.

A few years ago, I found myself behind on my patients' appointment times. This bothered the hell out of them, and it bothered the hell out of me as well.

I hated being behind on my appointments. It was not fair to anyone. As the years went by, I tried hard to be on time. I would not allow any of my staff to fool around with my scheduling book—like doubling up so that I wouldn't be idle. It didn't matter, because somehow there was always something that would throw the day into a spiraling spin toward earth.

There were many reasons that I would get behind on my appointments, and they all seemed to be beyond the control of myself and my staff. Someone would bring a family member with them to their appointment and decide that I should see that person as well. We would have a cancellation and fill in the spot.

I thought that none of this was our fault, but I knew it was our problem. As it turned out, it was mostly my fault and completely my problem.

Here is my solution, and after many tries, it works for everyone in my clinical practice. I work in my office from 8 a.m. until noon. If there is a cancellation in the schedule, it is left there as a potential hole. If I find myself without a patient for fifteen minutes, I walk around the building and chat with anyone willing to let me strike up a conversation. When I get beeped, I go back to work. From noon until two o'clock, I am free to take a nap, go to the gym to work out, go back to the hospital and make rounds, or whatever I need to do.

If I was up late the night before, I know that this schedule allows the luxury of napping. If I need to see someone who is in the hospital, I can go.

The other problem that needed solving was that of seeing "work-ins," people who need to see a doctor right away before we can accommodate them with an appointment. I promise my patients that no matter what, they will be seen the same day they call. When they call, they are told that I start my work-ins at two o'clock, and I will stay until they are seen. I take care of the immediate problem, and then move on to the next room.

It took me six and one-half years to crack this code. This system takes away much of the pressure that comes with being a solo practitioner. I'm happy. My staff is happy, and my patients are happy, and it's all because of this thing we call time. Instead of being out of it, I'm on it.

No, I'm Not Really Scared

Listen, I've got something to say.
OK.
I'm not sure, but there, well...
What?
Well, you see those tests I ran...
Well, what?
Bill, uh, I just want you to know that, uh...
So far Doc, you haven't told me anything.
I know I'm screwing this up, but it bothers the
hell outta me to have to tell you this.
How can you not be scared?
I'm just not.
There's got to be a reason.
There is, you see Doc, da da da da di da da da.
Ah.

When Bill came to me as a patient, I took an immediate liking to him. He had an infectious smile and personality. He was just an all-around nice guy, the good drinking buddy type. If he drinks, he'd probably be my drinking buddy. It took us a while to get to the reason why he came to me for medical advice, but after I had listened to some of his stories, I knew what was wrong with Bill.

Bill had several problems, but none of them were big ones, so I was always able to get him through whatever came up. On a routine examination,

I ordered some lab tests. When I got the results back I noticed some abnormalities, which worried me. I called Bill and told him to come to my office so I could go over the results with him. It looked very much like he had cancer, and I knew I needed to discuss the possibilities of what I could do for him.

Bill was a few years older than me, and was from the Vietnam order, so I felt that he had already been through some pretty raw deals.

While I was thinking about what I would say to Bill, I reflected back to a time when a wife of one of my patients had called to tell me that she knew her husband was dying. Immediately, I left the office and went over to their house, remembering the first time that those kind people had asked my wife and myself out to eat. We really had a great time with them.

There I was, going to the house of man who had terminal cancer, and I had no idea what I was going to do. I thought about the helplessness that lady had to be feeling. Shortly she would not be alone because I was on my way. They were very private people. So private that the man would never accept his rectal medications from me. When I arrived at their home, the man was very lethargic, and I did my job. I sat with the family, thinking about all of the sadness filling the room, because of this ritual called dying.

The man died a few hours later, and I felt honored to have been invited to share this crucially sad time with his family. I had also been given the chance to be involved with helping him through his pain, during his last few hours. I thought about what a neat man he was as I looked through the pictures his family brought out to show me. I think about him a lot. I had such a hard time telling him that his cancer had come back. Actually, he helped me more that day than I helped him.

It sounds like I'm a wimp, but I can't help it if I get close to my patients. I sometimes get so close to them that they can not only reach out and touch me, they can also reach out and slap me.

Now, back to the story. Bill came into my office, and I hoped that I would come across to him as a professional and not an idiot. The morning of his appointment, when I looked at the patient list and saw his name, I just stared at it and kept telling myself, "don't fumble your words, Dominick. Get to the point. Hell, you're the doctor. Do your job!

When I started to talk to Bill, I hemmed and hawed, just enough to sound real stupid. I tried desperately to tell him of my concerns, and he understood. He knew that the man who was standing across from him, holding a stethoscope in his hands, dressed in blue jeans and wearing running shoes, was his doctor and his friend.

"Nothing scares me," he said. That courageous comment threw me down onto a chair sitting nearby.

I said, "Bill, how in the world can you say that? Everyone is afraid of something."

He answered me with, "I used to be scared, but not anymore. When I was a kid I had some fears, but nothing major. Just the usual stuff. Then I went to 'Nam' and fought on the hill with my buddy. We took on some major heat from Charlie, and I was so scared that I couldn't control my bowels. As we were getting ready to get the hell outta there, I turned to my buddy just about the time that he took a hit, and he didn't have no head no more. Since then, I ain't never been scared."

Ah.

Hold On

But.. .but. . .but..
But, nothing!
Really, I'm not kidding.
You had your chance.
But...but...
What do you think you're doing, missy?
But, I asked you.
You should have...
Well, it's too late now.

When I was a student in grade school, I was thrilled to be learning and delighted that learning was so easy for me. I experienced growing up in the country much differently than my friends who lived in the city did. The school I attended was so small that there were only forty of us in my graduating class. We ran the bell curve, for what it's worth, but our training was similar to other schools, in many respects.

There was a tough kid I remember who went all the way through school with me, and he kept everyone at bay whenever he had the urge. I could never figure out why he couldn't seem to get along without using force. My growing up years went along smoothly for the most part, and I enjoyed being a kid immensely. My childhood was good because I never tried to make trouble, and I worked hard at making sure that I didn't.

I was glad to have a stay-at-home Mom, because when I would get home from school, she would be waiting for me to tell her about my day. Many times my Dad would come home early from work so he could spend more time with the family. My sisters and I fought all the time, but on our Thursday night family meetings, we would work through our differences (much like a confession, erasing the slate), and then we'd go right back to our normal bickering for another week.

When I was in the third grade, a girl in my class stood out in the crowd because she didn't act like the rest of us. She was different and because she was different, the kids would make fun of her. I guess they did that so they could feel better about themselves.

We came in from recess one day and were ready to hit the books. She asked the teacher for permission to go to the bathroom. That was a simple, innocent request, which deserved nothing less than a nod from the teacher, indicating to the girl that she had permission to be excused. Instead, Mrs. S went ballistic on her.

The girl never talked much, because she had learned through the years to keep a low profile so that she wouldn't encourage her classmates to start picking on her. They always managed to start picking on her, where they left off after each new activity would begin. I remember thinking, "Just let the poor girl go to the bathroom. It's absolutely harmless. What's the big deal?"

A few minutes went by, and the girl asked the teacher again. The teacher was very disturbed and abruptly told her, "No!" That teacher had a bad attitude.

I remember saying under my breath, "Please change your mind, Mrs. S, and let her go to the bathroom!"

A few more minutes went by and the distressed girl began urinating while sitting at her desk. Her pee ran down the floor, the kids started laughing, and Mrs. S started screaming. My heart and soul wept silently. I was so embarrassed for the girl that I thought I was going to die right there in my chair. That child was totally humiliated, and I knew it.

I didn't realize it then, but that girl had been labeled by society, as a throw-away kid. When I was in school there were no special provisions or classes to meet the needs of kids who were different. Today, most of the schools in America have classes for kids with special needs. So, what did society do to my classmate who was different? It swept her right under the rug, and educated the so-called normal kids without as much as a blink of an eye.

That was the way they acknowledged the fact that something wrong was going on.

I have a patient who is a special education teacher, and one day I told her my story and asked her why she chose to teach special children. She said, "I've always had the desire to help the less fortunate," and then she told me several experiences that had touched her heart, and when she left the office, I thought, "Wow. That patient of mine has some darn fortunate kids in her class, because she feels the pain of her students, and she has the driving force to help them."

I'm not quite sure what happened to the girl I've written about, but I still have a vivid memory of the pain I felt for her, and my prayer is, "God bless all of the children who are like her everywhere, and God bless the teachers that are teaching those children, and God bless the parents of those children, and God bless society for coming up with a special education program in the schools."

I'm not a perfect man by any means, and I'm the first to admit it, but I still feel anger toward Mrs. S. for the way she treated my classmate. She took a big chunk out of that little girl's soul, by humiliating her, over and over again in front of the whole class. I'm sorry for my soul, but I still can't say, "God bless Mrs. S."

First Day Back

Every time I take time out to go on a vacation, I feel anxious about the overwhelming amount of work that will be facing me when I return. As a general rule, on my first day back, my days are hectic, and I feel like I'm being pulled in all directions.

I usually take ten days off for my vacations, with two weekends tied together so that I don't miss too many days being away from my patients. My anxiety always occurs toward the end of my vacations. I start thinking too much about the mountain of paperwork and the problems that always pile up.

For some time now I have been suffering with burnout in my job. It seems I have no time for myself and never enough time for my family. When I go on vacations I do a lot of catching up, but it never seems like enough. It seems I inhale for many months, hold it, and then exhale for a week or so.

This pattern of living has been disheartening to me and caused me to get burned out with what I love to do. When I am on vacation, I spend much of the time trying to figure out where I am in my life and where I want to go. Those feelings are mixed with a healthy dose of wondering where I need to be and where I need to go. My needs and wants take over my mind.

Don't get me wrong. I'm not bitching. OK, I am bitching. I just get tired, just like everyone does. Before I take vacations I'm always tired and ready to give up. I'm human and that's what happens to humans.

I got back from my last vacation early on a Sunday afternoon. I knew I should go to my office and try to get ahead with my paperwork, but for some reason I couldn't do it. I could not, would not, should not and did not go to my office. Did I have anxiety feelings over my decision? Actually, no. Not that time. Why not? I'm not sure, but I think it had to do with the fact that I wasn't ready to give into the monster of a practice to control me.

On the following day I arrived at work about an hour earlier than usual so I could jump on the paperwork, and it wasn't as bad as I thought it was going to be. The doctor who had been covering for me while I was away had a long list of patients that he had admitted into the hospital, so I knew I would be very busy making hospital calls. Then my day at the office began.

My first patient of the day was a bit early. He was a young hypertensive man whom I had first seen at the burn unit. This man's medical condition was touch and go for almost two years. I remember him being on a respirator while he was in the burn unit, and how he almost didn't make it through his ordeal.

With the help of some great nurses and an outstanding burn surgeon, we were able to get the young man out of the hospital. While I was chatting with him that first day after my vacation, I reflected on what an important role I had played in getting him back to his family and job. I felt good about that.

My second patient was a New Yorker that could BS his way across America in less time than it takes to make a phone connection. I asked him about his wife because she was getting into some trouble with a relentless sinus infection before I'd left on vacation. It took several visits before we could get the right antibiotic to help her.

My patient told me that his wife was doing great and thanked me for asking. We chatted a while and had a nice visit. He assured me that he was going to quit smoking, but he couldn't right now. He told me that he was down from smoking two packs a day to only a half of a pack a day. I felt good about that.

My next patient was a lady I had not seen in a while. She had a lump in her neck that I had been worrying about for some time. The lump turned out to be caused from an upper airway infection. I prescribed some antibiotics and told her to come back in a month and I would recheck the lump, just to make sure. She was relieved. I felt good about that.

I saw patient after patient that day, and it made me feel good to be able to help them all. Before my vacation, I felt like I was really not helping anyone, but my first day back on the job proved me wrong. It made me feel good to be proved wrong, and especially that day, because I'd come to work feeling totally burned out.

At the end of the day I was handed a chart that had a message clipped to it about a patient who was very unhappy with me. I couldn't understand why. I had given her opportunity after opportunity to come to my office so I could help her, but she would always refuse to come in for her visits. No matter what I did for her, she would bitch about it. She knew she needed to have her medicines adjusted periodically but refused to come to the office. When we called her, she would say bad things about me and use her anger as an excuse. She loved to blame me for her not coming to my office.

Well, I sat down and typed a letter to the lady. That was my last order of the day. There was definitely a problem with the doctor-patient relationship, so I knew that I needed to try to fix it. I had already tried several times in the past. I had literally bent over backwards to help the lady, time after time, and each time she left me cleaning mud from my face. That's part of the reason I get burned out. It helps to have the kind of patients who really need me and understand the need to have their medicines reviewed. It's rewarding to have patients who want to come to me to have their heart and lungs checked to make sure that everything is going all right. Those are the patients that make my medical practice worthwhile and enjoyable.

As I was typing the letter, I knew what I had to tell her was long overdue.

Dear Madam:
You are obviously unhappy with me and therefore it is in your best interest that you find a new physician, etc...

I felt good about that.

You Must Have Been. . .

Oh, I could just see you now, Doctor.
See me what?
See you in school.
Yeah?
Yeah.
What do you see, ma'am?
Well, I see you so well behaved.
You do?
Yes, I do.
What else do you see, ma'am?
I see a bright little boy paying attention and
    doing what he's told.
Oh, yeah?
Yeah.
What if I told you different?
Well, I just wouldn't believe anything different.
Oh, yeah?
Yeah.

The course I dreaded the most was English. I studied a lot but somehow I couldn't grasp how many commas I needed or where to put the right things where they were supposed to be. In fact, almost every college subject left me cold except science. That was the subject where I really stood out. I felt that I could do anything if I mastered science.

But my professors told me that English was very important and they were going to prove it to me.

When I wrote my college term paper, I wrote about the Bermuda Triangle, and I researched it to the sky. I read twelve books on the subject. I did everything right to earn a good grade, except the number of commas. Consequently, I received a "D" on my project. It was humiliating to get a "D" on something I had spent so much time on. I was so angry that from then on I never tried to do well in any subject except my science courses.

For some reason God has sent me every retired English teacher who lives in my town. I have so many English teachers as patients that I can't even count them.

When I enrolled in medical school it was all science, and I was thrilled to no end! I regret not having cracked the code on being better at English as well as any with of the so-called liberal arts subjects. Sometimes I think I should go back to school and take a few liberal arts courses. I've even thought about trying out law school, but I'm not sure that I would be disciplined enough to follow through.

The Week I Was Ready to Quit

One week I had a fairly busy and rewarding week. I had a number of routine visits, and they went quite well. I'm glad things went so well for me, because until that week, I was ready to hang up my gloves. I was sure that there was no cure for burnout.

So many good things happened during the week that I was almost convinced to change my mind about quitting. Then at the end of the week, something very special happened to me that did change my mind. After that experience, I began to see things in a much better light.

My last patient of the day was a new patient nearly ninety years old. She was over-medicated—on several blood pressure medicines, and the doses were not fully maximized. It was a pinch of this and a pinch of that, but enough medicine to cost her a lot of money to keep up with this regimen. It was not only expensive; it was also difficult for her to keep up with scheduling the medicines.

Because of this lady's arthritic problems, I called my sister into the room to help me with some of the positioning. With love and care, we both helped this lady, and when all was said and done, she thanked us just for caring.

She was excited because she had found someone who would not only take care of her but someone who would listen to her as well. She said until that day she felt she had never been examined thoroughly enough by any doctor. Now she knew she was going to get back on track.

As a physician, I welcomed her thankfulness because I knew she was sincere. My sister felt good about it because she is a caring person and really gets involved with helping the patients. The moment was especially nice for me because it was at the end of my week, and I was almost ready to give up. I had been feeling like no one really cared if I helped them or not. When I thought about that nice lady thanking me and being so grateful for my care, I realized that I shouldn't have felt so defeated because I have so many patients who are thankful for my care and allow me to serve them.

After that experience, I started to get the fire back under my skin so that I could go on with my practice and take good care of my patients. I hope God will keep me going and grant me many more rewarding days in my practice, and I hope my patients know that I care.

Please, Let the Doctor Diagnose

I found out in a way I would have never dreamed possible that the saying, "a little bit of knowledge can be dangerous," is true. I have always believed in the philosophy that I know what I know, and I know what I don't know. Anything outside of those boundaries is ignorance. I stay inside the lines. That is the only way I can protect my patients from some other person's ignorance.

Mrs. X was a demanding patient with a problem. She had gotten her liver into trouble because of drinking too many gin and tonics, and now she was paying the price. From her examination I found she had a clear chest, a strong heart, a large abdomen, and very swollen feet. She was examined by a surgeon who felt that she had gone a bit too far with her habits for him to try and correct anything without her dying on the operating table. Mrs. X was not particularly thrilled to get such news, but she accepted it.

While she was a patient in the hospital, she was being seen by a physical therapist. I don't remember the reason for her therapy, but I do remember vividly something that happened while I was making my hospital rounds. An incredibly hostile group of family members was waiting for me in Mrs. X's room. When I walked into the room, they flew into me like they were going to stone me with the kind of stoning that you can read about in the Bible.

"What kind of doctor are you?" one of family members asked. "You have no idea what you're doing to our mother. We found out from the physical therapist what's wrong with her. How can we get another doctor now, today?"

I was shocked. My eyebrows probably flew away from the force of the gale wind. I had no idea what the lady was talking about. I said, "What did the therapist tell you?"

The lady answered, "She told us that our mother is in heart failure, and that is why her legs are swollen."

That therapist cost me forty-five minutes of my time having to explain to Mrs. X as well as all of her family members that she did not have heart failure. I told them that there were more ways than one to get swollen feet. The entire time I was thinking, "How could you people believe a physical therapist's diagnosis over your doctor's?"

The reality of any medical situation is that when a person is sick there is not much of a chance of reversing the mechanism that got them there. It is a doctor's job to grab out for anything that will help to get his or her patient well. Mrs. X hadn't remembered that I told her I had thoroughly checked out her heart and because she didn't remember, she hadn't told anyone in her family.

The forty-five minutes the therapist cost me was not the important issue. It was the trust she took away from my patient and her family members. Things were never the same after that no matter how much explaining I did. The physical therapist somehow had failed to learn what she didn't know, and a lot of people got hurt.

They Can't All Love You

They're not all going to love you, kid.
Why not?
'Cause that's the way it goes.
I don't understand.
It doesn't matter. Not everyone is gonna like you.
But, what if I do everything I'm supposed to do?
It doesn't matter.
You're kidding?
Nope, I'm not kidding.
I don't believe you.
It's OK, but you'll see that I'm right.
No, you'll see that I'm right.
Wanna bet?
No, not really.

It's always been important to me to be liked. This is not one of those psychological things, just something everyone wants and needs—positive feedback, as they say. When I first started my medical practice, I tried in every way to prove that everyone was going to like me. I knew I was the only one responsible for this happening, so if it didn't, it was my fault, of course.

It didn't take long before I found out just how wrong I had been. Every time I heard some comment about me that was less than flattering, it would kill me. "How could someone say something like that?" I thought. Sometimes, as smart as I think I am, there must be a dumb Dominick inside of me somewhere just to keep me balanced.

Not every doctor is the right one for every patient, and many people find that truth out the hard way. I digress.

Some time ago I heard a conversation about whether or not someone liked a particular place to live. In the conversation statements were made about the pros and cons, but mostly cons, about the place where I am living.

My wife and I have decided to play up the pros in such conversation and to let others know that we are quite content living where we are. That was a lesson learned. I also learned that even if you could place some people in the lap of luxury, their bitch motors will still find the juice and power to run incessantly.

I'm not saying that I am the best at anything or that I cannot make mistakes. What I am saying is that I have learned to do what I believe is right and go with that at face value.

The society we live in has a big problem with abuse, mostly with the abuse of females. It is heart-breaking to see some of the abuse women have endured in the past and continue to endure today.

Some time ago I heard about a "bitchy daughter" of a woman who was not my patient. She threw the wrench in at every turn because she had to be sure that her terminally ill father would not come off of his life support. I was told that she was extremely well informed with regard to the futility of his care continuing and that everything had been done appropriately. The war dance continued. Nothing was going to change that lady's mind.

No one could say for sure exactly what was going through her mind, but it was blatantly clear that this lady was hurting. Who was going to help her with her pain? She wasn't a bitch, she was a victim.

I wonder if all she wanted was to know why she had been abused by the man that she called Daddy. If that was all she needed to know, it seemed to me that she had missed the critical period in which to ask it.

As a good nation we must take steps to stop this unaccountable behavior. Abusive acts only destroy and never heal. We need to hold our little girls in our arms and love them.

Stop and think about your dialogue with your family. Sometime ago I heard that a man should treat his wife the way he would want his mother, or the mother of his children, treated. That says it best. Being a good man doesn't mean that all you have to do is bring home the bacon. It means that you should come home and play with your kids and love your wife. Don't go out and have a beer with your buddies after work. Go home and have a pop and fries with your wife and kids. Go home to supper.

Just a few days ago while my son and I were stopped at a stoplight, he said, "Frosty the Snowman got into trouble because he didn't understand the stoplight signals, Daddy."

The same evening my daughter had to be taught that "four" was not just a number, but also something that explained "for" this and "for" that;

both words just happen to sound the same. I am thankful that I was there to be a part of these experiences with my kids—truly the highlight of my day.

I know that I lack many qualities that keep me from being the perfect husband and father. That truth keeps me working at trying to better myself each day. My self-expectations are not for me to be a great man, whatever that is, but for me to be a good man.

Getting back to the "bitchy daughter". . . I am sorry for whatever happened to her. I am sorry that she'll go to her grave never knowing that what happened to her was not her fault. It hurt her not to have been hugged when she should have. She felt pain when she should have felt good.

When I was in training to become a doctor, I learned from a psychiatrist to always ask my patients about abuse and to ask whether it took place when they were children or after they had become adults. He told me that I would have a lot of women patients who had been battered by their husbands. That psychiatrist was right.

When battered women come to me for medical help, they lift up a lifetime of stomach pains and headaches as they tell me stories they have to get off of their chest about their abuse. You may not understand this, but if you do I hope it will help you. I am writing this for you. Blessed are the children.

It Just Seems Like Yesterday

(A Dialogue Between a Doctor and His Patient)

Patient: Did you know that I was legally blind?
Doctor: No, ma'am, I didn't.
Patient: Well, I am, but that's not so bad.
Doctor: How do you feel now, ma'am?
Patient: I have a bit of a headache and my back still hurts; that's why I'm here in the first place.
Doctor: Yes ma'am, I know that. How long have you been having those headaches, ma'am?
Patient: Not long. They come and go. It's my back that's the real problem.
I guess at eighty I should expect some problems with my back.
But you know, I never expected to be legally blind. No siree, I never counted on that one, but I'm here just the same. Here's a list of my allergies and these are the meds I'm on.
Doctor: Do you live with your husband, ma'am?
Patient: Yes, I live with my husband. Thank God he's still around. You know, I don't know

what I'd do without him. His back's not great, either, but we both have more important things to be grateful for than reasons to complain.

Doctor: Do you smoke, ma'am?

Patient: No, I never smoked. I never drank either.

Doctor: Is there any cancer or heart diseases in your family history, ma'am?

Patient: No, none of those things are in my family history. Boy, you sure ask a lot of questions. An internists, is that what you call yourself?

Doctor: Yep, you're right. Do you have any brothers or sisters, ma'am?

Patient: No, I never had any brothers or sisters. I had a lot of cousins that would be sent home at the end of the day. Thank God for that.

Doctor: How many times have you been pregnant, ma'am?

Patient: How many times was I pregnant? Two times.

Doctor: Are your children alive and well, without health problems, ma'am?

Patient: I'm sorry for crying, but you really struck a chord there. I lost my precious little girl when she was only three days old. She was so beautiful. She had all of her fingers and toes. Everything seemed so perfect. She looked just like her father. It still hurts. I've never stopped thinking about her. It's been about sixty years now.

I Have Enough To Eat

When I began my practice I started getting gifts around the holidays from some of the physicians I referred my patients to as a Thank You for considering them. I never passed my patients around in the political arena of medicine in order to get referrals back. When I found a highly qualified physician I knew would do a good job taking care of my patients, I would hang onto that doctor for referrals.

I would never send one of my patients to a doctor that I wouldn't go to myself. I received roasted turkeys, chocolates, decorated cookies and more edible things than one could possibly imagine. Most of the goodies found their place on different peoples' tables because I was not in need of any of this. It was a case of the "haves" giving more to the "haves," which didn't seem quite right. It is still difficult for me to sit down to a delicious holiday meal without worrying about the people who are going hungry and doing without.

Fortunately, I came across an idea while reading that allows a way of sharing to come into the picture. Based on this concept, I wrote the following message, "Sharing Our Gifts." It was printed in the medical society bulletin.

Dominick Acquaro, M.D.

Sharing Our Gifts

Every year we are given the opportunity to share our gifts with others during the Christmas season. That is the time when we pass out our gifts to our family, our friends and our colleagues, hoping that our gifts are special to each one.

While I was contemplating this article, I remembered a children's book that I had read, "The Giving Tree," by Shel Silverstein. "The Giving Tree" is a story that teaches us unconditional love and the true gift of giving.

This story tells of a small boy who met unconditional love in a tree. He goes throughout his whole life with the tree always being there for him.

In the beginning of the story, the child needs shade, a place to swing and food to eat and the tree always gave him what he needed. The tree gave him a house to live in, and as he got older the tree gave him a boat so he could travel afar. Finally, near the end of their time together, the tree had become a mere stump and the boy had turned into an aged old man. Now it was time for the tree to give the aged old man its final gift. That gift was a place for the man to rest his weary head upon.

We meet many people in our lives who are givers, along with the blessed needy who need our gifts, because without them, they cannot thrive. In our personal lives, we give our families the basic needs that everyone requires. We give them a place to live, food to eat and clothes to wear. We give our children an education, hoping that they in turn will learn to give back to our society, the gift of giving, which is the most precious commodity of all. Whatever gifts they choose to give, whether they be the gift of themselves, or money, or education, or any other resources they may possess, their gifts of giving, will prove to be invaluable.

There are many people in this world who are in want and who need our open hearts, in order to survive. We were taught early in our lives to give selflessly and not to expect anything in return. But somewhere back in our minds, we usually do look for something in return. We are inclined to look for that warm glow that seems to fill our hearts when we have shared with others.

Even with our children we look for that feeling of pride when we are allowed to share the spotlight when they have accomplished something. All the while when we are doing our fine deeds, there is an avoidance system at work. We don't want anyone close to us to bring failures our way.

In fact, religion plays a big part in keeping us on the straight and narrow. I call this bargain giving. All around us we see people giving their time and money to churches and to specific charities, such as the March of Dimes and United Way. We learned this form of bargain giving from our religious ties when we were young. In a sense, bargain giving makes us feel like we are bargaining with higher powers, which puts us in the position of needing instead of giving.

When we give to the homeless and starving people, our humanistic feelings add to the religious overtones. But no matter what reasons we might have, there are really no bad reasons to give when someone is in need.

Occasionally, we take our own gift giving for granted and when we do, there always seems to be some power on our side that puts us back between the yellow lines. In keeping with the religious aspect of my train of thought, I want to share with you the fact that I am a recovering Catholic.

As a child, my parents had us toe the line. They expected us to do all of the right things that a Catholic was supposed to do. I felt that with as many masses as I attended I was good for at least a few decades!

My wife and I decided, after being given the gift of our children, that it was time for us to go back to church. As a recovering Catholic, I am still not the best church goer, but when I do go to church, and for as long as my son permits me to, I listen. On one particular Sunday, I remember a sermon that covered the subject of heaven and hell. That sermon really struck home with me, and if you don't mind, I would like to share it with you.

"A Saint was visiting hell and as he was looking around, he saw a beautifully decorated table with people sitting all around it, and there was too much food on the table to believe. He also noticed that everyone had five-foot-long forks. It was obvious to him that there was no way that the people who were sitting around the table, could feed themselves with such a large fork. As he looked around, all he could see was the strained looks of pain and suffering in those poor starving individuals' expressions. It was truly hell to have such a magnificent feast nearby and to have no way to eat the meal. Instantly, the man was escorted to Heaven. Again, he saw the exact same table, with the same feast on the table, and people sitting all around it. He noticed that those people had the same five-foot-long forks, but as he stood there, he noticed an obvious difference. He noticed that everyone who was sitting around the table, looked healthy and happy, because they were sharing their gift of giving, by feeding each other!"

As I listened to this sermon, I knew I wanted my gifts to be given in more of a personal way. So, that very day, I gave to my family the gift of myself. I promised them that I would give them my time and my listening ear. To the hungry, the homeless, and even the abused in our society, I promised to give a gift in the form of money to various charities, in honor of my friends and colleagues.

That was my way of showing my thankfulness for the many beautiful gifts I've shared in delightful conversations, for the generous gifts so many people have bestowed upon me, and for the many people who have given me the chance to practice medicine in a wonderful community. I hope you all have joyous giving during the holiday season of every year that you live!

The Downs Syndrome Child

On a cold and dark April morn
To anxious parents, a child was born.
She cried the usual cry and cooed the usual
coo.
She made all the usual sounds and made the
usual do.
It had been a particularly tough winter on them
As they peered through the glass and grinned
ear to ear.
They talked and held hands, as if they first met.
All those years of waiting, and she's finally
ours.
Does anyone in your family have that fold near
the eyes?
You know, her tongue doesn't seem to fit her
mouth.
They continued to smile.
You know the other mothers have already
gotten their baby.
What's going on with ours?
They walked to their room and all sat around
While the doctor explained this thing they
called Downs.
A perfect life she could live, but perfect for
whom?

She cried the usual cry and cooed the usual coo
She made the usual sounds and made the usual do.
I love you Paul.
And I love you, too.
Do you think we'll get through this?
I don't know.
Many Aprils passed, and then
They laid her to rest, 'neath the sun and the moon.
He sent for her here, but it just seemed too soon.
They sat in the park for hours, it seemed.
They sat in the park and they dreamed and they dreamed

One day as I was entering one of my examining rooms in my office, I saw a beautiful couple standing next to a precious nonverbal Downs child in a wheelchair. That child definitely needed medical attention. Her parents were looking at her like she was the only child in the whole wide world, and I couldn't help but think how lucky that child was to have those two loving individuals as her parents. They were undoubtedly the best Mom and Dad that anyone would ever want.

The child I'm writing about was nearly fifty years old and she was sitting in her wheelchair, sticking her oversized tongue out at me. She was as frightened as any young child would be when they are in a doctor's office. Her parents looked as worried as any new parents would look. They had every reason to be worried because on the least bit of exertion, she would become short of breath.

I realized the gravity of situation while I was examining her, and my heart went down to my feet. The parents told me that they never thought of having any more children after she was born because they knew that taking care of her would be a lifetime commitment. They told me that they were also afraid to have another child, and they said, "I hope you understand, doctor. We're not sorry for making that decision, but you know why, doctor, don't you?"

"I understand completely," I said.

As big as the child's heart was in kindness, it was even bigger in heart failure. There was very little anyone could do. It was time for me to educate the parents with some painful medical realities. The parents wanted their little girl fixed up so that she could get back to her normal self, and I knew that would not be possible.

It is important for doctors to recognize the limitations of medicine, and it's even more important for doctors to share their knowledge with their patients. doctors do not know everything, so they should not pretend that they do. Unfortunately, a lot of people think that a doctor can fix everything.

I will never take away hope from a patient, nor will I ever give false hope to a patient, but I will always do the best that I can to help a patient.

That precious child died. I did educate the parents on a few reasonable expectations, and they seemed to understand. I wrote the above poem just a few days after I had seen the Downs child in my office and a just a few weeks before she died. The words came directly from my heart. I didn't know her long, but I'll know her forever, now, in my memories.

The Last to Know

What is that?
Don't know.
What's it look like?
Don't know.
What do you think it is?
Don't know.
You're not blind.
Not stupid either.
Whatcha mean?
Just that.
That is stupid.
Not to me it's not.
It is what it is.
I agree with that.
Oh you finally agree.
Not cause you said it.
You've got a lot of doubt.
Maybe.
What else you got?
Some benefit.

Whenever I read a book I think might help my patients in certain situations, I pass it along to them. I do the same for the staff working with me in the office. Life doesn't come with a handbook, and if you don't search for answers to problems they usually go unsolved. This adds to your attic of hidden things, things you intend to do tomorrow but carry around forever. No one seems to clean out their attic and resolve things. This takes thought processing and concentration.

In my field of medicine you have to think of less obvious things. If it appears to be black, is it? If it appears to be white, is it? Is it both? Is it gray or is it just black and white?

Sometimes a patient gives me clues as to something else is going on. You have to read people. You have to also know that people have to be heard. Feelings have to be acknowledged and dealt with.

There is a lot of anger that manifests itself in many different forms. In psychology they teach us that love can be a manifestation of anger or hate toward someone. This kind of love somehow keeps the person who is despised safe from the one who hates.

We protect ourselves with our thoughts. We believe what is of benefit to us in a time and place. If you have ever talked about someone behind their back and betrayed them, don't you believe that the same will come right back at you? When you slight someone don't you believe it never goes completely unnoticed? Have you ever seen a child try to bend the truth and look at you, believing in his mind that he just invented lying?

Have you ever had friends who are so nice to you that you wonder where the heck are they coming from? You ignore this thought, tending to believe they are nice because it's you. Who wouldn't be nice to a person like you? You're the best thing that has ever happened to them. Everybody would die to be your friend.

Have you ever had a friend that pulled no punches and just told everything like it was? Called a jack a jack. You don't even worry where you stand with them. You may feel a little uneasy, but you're not in the dark.

You don't always have to agree with people. Nothing in the rule books says that. It is nice when you're not able to be in agreement but are able to be in understanding.

My sister who works in my office came to me one day livid because someone had told her that one of the doctors I refer my patients to was ill-mannered. I had heard this from patients before and understood that although ill-mannered, he was an excellent doctor.

Now I saw the other side. I listened to the complaints and walked through this with my patients.

My sister (who, by the way, thinks she is the boss) threatened to not let any of my patients go to that physician. This obviously is a little out of the pecking order and would never happen. I knew it was time to let her in on the less obvious. This doctor had recently lost a child to death, and a rare blood cancer was soon to take his wife.

His role as a doctor must have been clouded by his role as a father, a husband and household provider. Right or wrong, he had other things on his mind. He couldn't practice medicine with a smile on his face, but he could still practice good medicine. He just couldn't be the comforter when he was in need of being comforted.

Soft-liners would offer the "God bless this poor man's soul," as my sister did when she knew.

Hard-liners would say, "Well, why don't he just take some time off until he deals with this?"

Between these extremes we would have comments that would range from the east to the west and all points in between. Nothing makes everything right. There is not a one-size-fits-all answer. If you cannot find grounds to be in agreement with another person, at least try to find grounds to be understanding. This would be a good thing to share.

Where Did All the Used Station Wagons Go?

Value this and value that.
Is anyone listening?
Hey I said value this and value that.
OK.
How come you're not listening?
Value schmalue.
Hey!
Well what about this and what about that?
What about it?
You buyin'?
Nope.
Why not?
Why should I?
You make me sick.
You make me sicker.
I see the poke.
What?
I see the poke.
And...
And when you speak I smell the pig.

It seems that everyone has an angle. Well, not really, because we don't do things the same way. We are different in many respects. Even though we are different we are approached in much the same way. Most of us watch television, read the newspaper, look at billboards as we drive. . .

Many times I will sit and listen to a patient tell me about a child who is going through a divorce. It's usually the mother telling me about this, because we men don't as a rule talk about such things. There are usually a lot of tears and a lot of trying to understand why this is happening.

These parents are hurting terribly for their child. A lot of times they will say that they thought the most difficult times of raising their child was over. They now realize that it is just beginning. As time passes they heal a little but not a lot.

My patients teach me a lot about life. Sometimes after I have read a rewarding book, I'll share this with my patients and try to help them this way. Many times it works.

As I was growing up we always had a dog. We took some responsibility for this dog but for the most part he or she was on his or her own. They took their life into their own hands at our house.

Our society seems to be in a buying frenzy. Buy bigger and faster no matter what it costs you. Even if it costs your life. When I started practice, the residency program in my town allowed all the residents to moonlight from the first year. As I watched the parking lot it would grow with foreign sports cars during the first half of each fiscal residency year.

I felt that was OK because I have my toys as well. I've managed to buy nice cars but at a fraction of their original cost. I never buy new for me. When you work hard for many years in school and you feel the need to reward yourself there is nothing wrong with buying things you want. Enjoy.

I read a lot of books about how to manage this or that in one's life. Rarely have I been enlightened so much that I would need fluids through my veins to pull me out of shock. We all make our fair share of mistakes, but we also manage to pull ourselves back to the tracks and continue the journey—hopefully.

I watch television carefully. The other day I watched a commercial about money lending. As a home owner, turn that money into a dreamboat, a vacation, whatever. All I heard was that if you were in a hole and barely surviving—Hey! Let us dig it a little deeper and snuff the life right out of you.

We are not watching programs; we are being programmed. We are being approached, legally, to pull every dime from our pockets and lay it out. It's the American way. People are trying to give their children what they didn't have when they should be giving them what they had—their mothers at home.

As I look back and try to think how I would change anything about growing up, I realize there's nothing I would change. We had a used station wagon and our mother at home. At the time I wanted things, but even sheiks in foreign lands are in want of things. We had our mother. What more could you ask for?

As the entertainment media grow more aggressive with their attempts to empty pockets, our mothers across the land spill out of the house and into the streets into new minivans. They drop the children of America into the laps of the barely known to be cared for until the quitting time buzzer goes off. Who is raising our children?

Buy way under what you can afford, and you might be able to find a nice used car somewhere. If you're really lucky it might be a station wagon. The trade-off? Instead of giving kids what you didn't have, you give them what you did have (if you were lucky). You.

You, whether you're a mom or a father mom or any other combination. When you see the politicians talking the talk on family values you might recognize that you are the ones who are walking the walk. You can certainly tell if they are not walking the walk. Don't be fooled by rhetoric.

If you see that poke held up for you and you hear squealing, don't take a whiff.

It's OK to reward yourself, but don't yield to gluttony. Have a healthy but satiable appetite. Enjoy life and your family and don't give them up for anything. Despite appearance, the grass is never greener on the other side. Learn to appreciate what you have and what you're able to afford. Don't lose out on family values. Don't lose out on love or life.

You can't lose what you don't have. If you have a family keep it. If you overspend, don't let this interfere with raising your children. You can always take that new car back. You cannot get back the time your child spent in a day care being raised by someone else.

Your child doesn't want what you didn't have.

Bless your child with what you did have and turn that television off.

Keith

Dear Keith,
I think about you often.
You're probably wondering why I haven't called.
How's the family?
Doesn't seem so long ago does it?
I drive through Chicago often.
I'll probably stop next time I'm in.
Anything new?
I'll probably not send this letter.
Maybe I'll get by there soon.
Maybe it will be like old times.
Can't be too old huh?
Heck we're only forty-three.
Forty-three. That's not old is it Keith?
How's your family?
Well gotta go.
Busy you know.
Too busy to live sometimes.
Heck I'll probably see you soon.
Love Dom.

Life is good. I've been reading about how to be a better person for many years. It's not that I consider myself a person that needs betterment. I consider betterment for the good of all persons. We just do it differently. Some a lot and some not at all.

I met my dear friend Keith in the eighties. He served at that time in the hospital where I was training as a teaching cardiologist. One day I was waiting in the radiology department when he walked in beside his partner and was introduced to me as one of "Y'all."

His partner, who was not a native of this land, spoke with a very strong accent and seemed to be intrigued with my Southern accent. It turned out that Keith and I had grown up in the Carolinas not very far from each other.

If you're from the South you'll understand this. For some reason we're always being told we're slow. We're always being asked about the Civil War and what do grits really taste like.

Keith was dressed in one heck of a suit, and I couldn't help wondering how comfortable he really was. I was two months his senior in age, but he was a teaching cardiologist and I was a first year resident.

I was very low on the food chain.

Keith taught me about much more than cardiology. He taught me about how to set up and run a practice. He taught me how to eat greasy fried catfish out of a bucket. The key was that you needed a bucket of beer beside you. Now are these not important lessons?

We used to get together and play Pictionary. Keith and I had a way of barely getting things down on paper with that game and *knowing* right away what the other was thinking. I remember "sonic boom' as one of those phrases where the lead barely hit the paper and the other knew.

He taught me how life was good and that two Southern boys could enjoy the heck out of Chicago together. Our wives were good friends and we all had fun together.

I left Chicago some nine years ago now and remember our good times as if they were yesterday. We've gotten together only a few times since Chicago and I keep promising myself that the next time I go through that town I'm gonna look that boy up, and we'll have some catfish and beers.

Two nights ago I got a call from his wife. Keith had died early that afternoon. He had been sick for some time. If you check my phone bills you wouldn't find his number on it for a long time back. If you checked my heart you would. I loved Keith and respected him. I'm going to miss him terribly.

I knew Keith had been sick, but the last time I'd heard I thought he was doing much better. He taught me that you could be quite sick and still laugh and play. I thought it was all the catfish and beers that were making us sick, but I was the only one that got better.

My daughter and son had their first communion, and I had to get a new suit as the ones I had were a bit too small. My daughter went to confession and then it was my son's turn. When the priest asked him what sins he had, he pointed to his sister and said, "Same as hers. If she hits me I hit her back."

It was a beautiful suit, and I remembered thinking that I hoped that every time I put it on I would be that happy.

I called Paul, a mutual friend of ours from Chicago, and shared the sad news with him. We were both very fond of Keith. Paul told me he would get the information we needed and get back in touch. I told Paul I loved him and in echoing this to me he suggested that we learn a lesson from this and get together soon.

Keith was a good man and he fought a hard fight. Even in his death he has taught me a lesson. Wherever he ends up I wonder if they'll have cat-fish and beer. Who knows maybe by the time we get together again it might be all gone.

Love Dom.

Bob

Where you from, ma'am?
Gravel Switch.
You're kiddin'!
Nope.
Who in the world would name a place that?
Don't know.
What's your name?
Anna Mae.
Your Mama named you that?
Yep.
Where is Gravel Switch?
Kentucky.
You grow up there?
Yep.
In a big family?
Yep.
How many?
Lots.
What was it like growing up there?
Good.
Good?
Yep. Good. Real good.
You mean no city folk?
I didn't say that.
Then what?
Just good.
What you doing 'round these parts?

Family business.
What kind of business?
You mean, What kind of family?
Yep.
My baby brother.
What you doing here with your baby brother?
I've come to bury him.
I'm sorry.
So am I.

My sister works in my office, and for some reason refers to me on varied occasions as a redneck. She knows I'm not a racist. She knows I may drink some beer but mostly it's because I'm working on my cars and trying to muscle them up.

There was a kid in school with a '64 Chevy that was muscled up. I always remember this car. I would have died to have it. I never stopped being a car hound and am stuck in the sixties with visions of Mopars and Chevies bouncing through my head.

Anyway, the term "redneck" is used with gentle loving care, or it darn well better be.

Some years ago Pat, a worker in my office, would ride me that we needed another person there. I would try to blow her off and get her to understand my way of thinking. She never did, of course, but it was a nice sparring event just the same.

In my first office a lady next door worked for a large office and was as nice as she could be. She later became my patient and was just the kind of person everyone took up with right away.

There was only one problem about her working for me. She needed two months off every year.

Still, she was worth the hassle. A smoker's laugh filled with life, if you could imagine one. To this day I envy the way she enjoys life. I'm always trying to figure out her secret.

Years ago she married and then was widowed at a young age. Her start was as an only child, but now she was responsible for three only children. I doubt she ever walked twenty miles through the snow to buy eggs, but she didn't have it easy, either.

Her next husband came along later when she was older and wiser, at least older. We all heard about him before we met him and loved him from the start. He was a kind, passionate sort with no particular mission other than keeping the peace at home. He was a Southern boy who could skin a critter and cook it if he had to.

Every year we have a Christmas party at my house, and every year we enjoy his stories.

Living in the city or the suburbs thereof, it would be hard to find the following scenario.

Here comes a 'possum for this man to see in my front yard. Under his direction, we follow him out to the front yard. He came what I would consider dangerously close to this creature. He played with it as if they both understood each other as family. My children were getting a nice lesson and so were the rest of us. Life was good.

He had a dog he loved dearly, and even though it wasn't what a group of polled people would call a "man's dog," it was this man's dog. This man, who had played college ball and proven himself on many a playing field. This also included the armed services. He was a man with his dog. He would come and pick up his wife and wait for her patiently outside by a picnic table, harmlessly flirting with a woman his wife called "Barbie." Life was good.

Their two-month trip came and went, and everyone was excited as usual to see them return. He'd had some trouble on the trip but as usual played everything down. By the time he came to see me as a patient, he was in heart failure. It was a Monday, and his symptoms were a few weeks old. He knew and had known for a long time from his heart doctors that he had a bad heart. Was he holding out for one last hurrah?

Immediately he was placed in the hospital, a sick man. Life was beginning to be not so good. Things happened fast, and everything failed. Life was not good at all. Bob was dying. I couldn't save him. All the team of doctors couldn't save him.

As Bob went through the dying process we all began our grieving process. Ana Mae came, and I met her. A sweet big sister. In the office we all had a wonderful person losing her husband. We all grieved in our own way.

The day Bob died, no one was ready—as usual.

His funeral came, and a hired preacher who didn't know Bob said some words I felt were not worthy of Bob. He needed more. He was a redneck in the nicest sense. He had showed us all how to capture a 'possum. We all loved Bob, and we all love Sondra today.

If I were to guess back to the day I was born I don't believe that a day when a girl named Ana May was saying good-bye to her little brother Bob would have been in the cards for me.

And who would have guessed they would be from Gravel Switch, Kentucky?

I Didn't Realize

I didn't realize.
Maybe you didn't.
No, I didn't.
Well, just in case explain.
Explain what?
You talk about darkness.
Yeah?
It's a downer.
For whom?
For everyone.
You say this.
Yeah.
We learn through sadness.
But we avoid sadness.
Yeah.
What should we do?
Not sure.
Life is a celebration.
As is death.
So.
So it has to do with life.
Do all your patients die?
What kind of question is that?
It sounds so depressing.
It is.
But should you be talking about this?
Why not?

Let someone else do it.
But we wait and wait.
So.
So.
I don't think you understand me.
I don't think you understand me.
Well, where do you see yourself a hundred years
from now?
Dead.
Well, wouldn't you want that to be a pleasant
experience?
Yes.
What is so bad about talking about this?
It's like picking out a coffin.
It's like a part of life?
Yeah.
Yeah.
You can't appreciate happy without sad,
can you?
I'm just trying to say I care.
I know you do.
You do?
I do.
Yeah.
Yeah.

We all see the world from our own lookout tower. I hope that this book helps you to enjoy your physician and care for each other. There are a lot of questions I see raised every day that I continue to write about and try to help with. If you have any suggestions or questions, I'll be glad to address them in the future.

Bedside Matters—Thanks for listening!